SOCIAL ASPECTS

OF

CHRISTIANITY.

SOCIAL ASPECTS

OF

CHRISTIANITY

BY

BROOKE FOSS WESTCOTT, D.D., D.C.L.

CANON OF WESTMINSTER

AND REGIUS PROFESSOR OF DIVINITY, CAMBRIDGE.

SECOND EDITION.

Wipf & Stock

PUBLISHERS

Eugene, Oregon

πεπλήρωται ὁ καιρός, καὶ ἤγγικεν ἡ βασιλεία τοῦ θεοῦ. μετανοεῖτε καὶ πιστεύετε ἐν τῷ εὐαγγελίῳ.

St Mark i. 15.

First Edition **1887**
Second Edition **1888**

Wipf and Stock Publishers
199 West 8th Avenue, Suite 3
Eugene, Oregon 97401

Social Aspects of Christianity
By Westcott, B.F.
ISBN: 1-59244-510-1
Publication date 1/29/2004
Previously published by Macmillan and Co., 1888

PREFACE.

THE Sermons in the present volume were preached (with two exceptions) during my residence at Westminster in August and December, 1886. I have indeed endeavoured to enforce the main ideas which they contain at various times during the last thirty years; but the opportunity seemed to require that I should endeavour to bring, as far as I could, into a clear and connected form what had been spoken only fragmentarily before. No one indeed can tell what is the effect which 'the Abbey' and the vast congregations which gather there, eager to listen, produce upon one who first experiences it at the close of life. Of all places in the world 'the Abbey,' I think, proclaims the social Gospel of Christ with the most touching eloquence.

So it was that when I was called to work at Westminster in 1884 I could not but feel with intense force the power of old thoughts, and in the first sermon of my first residence I indicated a line of teaching which I hoped to pursue if the time were given. Some passages from that Sermon will serve as an introduction to what follows.

When we are by the force of circumstances, or more truly by the loving providence of God, brought face to face with a great fact, a great duty, a great idea, and stand as it were alone in its presence, we are, I fancy, startled to find how little we have ever really thought upon it, how slenderly we are prepared to give any account of its relation to ourselves. We grow familiar with traditional criticisms: we adopt conventional customs: we repeat popular phrases; but all these lie for the most part outside our own actual experience: we have not made them our own by resolute reflection and self-questioning. The fact, the duty, the idea, is itself strange to us.

Is not this true of that which is for each one of us the greatest fact, the greatest duty, the greatest idea, life itself? How few of us pause even at such a time and in such a place as this to consider what life is, not in its circumstances but in its energy, in its capacities, in its issues. We all know, even if the knowledge has little practical effect, that no measure of time or sense gives a standard of its value. Life is more than the sum of personal enjoyments and pains through which it finds expression; more than the length of days in which it is visible to human eyes; more than the fulness of means which reveals to us its power. All these pass away, but in the process of their vanishing a spiritual result has been fulfilled. The soul of the man has been brought into fellowship—a fellowship welcomed or disregarded—with men and with the world and with God. It has consciously or unconsciously learnt much and done much. It has shaped a character for itself; it has helped to shape a character for others. It is at the end, most solemn thought, 'as it has been used.' *Life* then, we can see, *consists not in abundance*, in the overflowing richness of unemployed resources: it springs not spontaneously *from the things which we possess*, from our original endowments, as the necessary product of natural gifts. It is the opportunity of the individual to win for God by God's help that which lies within his reach: to accomplish on a scale little or great the destiny of humanity as it has been committed to him: to consecrate, it may be, splendid wealth to common service: to transfigure sordid cares by a divine vision: to rise to the truth of the Incarnation as the revelation of the purpose of the Father for the world which He made.

Life, in a word, as has been most nobly said,

> Life, with all it yields of joy and woe,
> And hope and fear,
> Is just our chance o' the prize of learning love,
> How love might be, hath been indeed, and is.

Now it is here, I believe, in this view of life realised among us, of life as individual in its responsibility and social in its aims, that we shall find the sure hope of a solution of the terrible riddles of existence which meet us on all sides. The overwhelming sorrows by which we are surrounded and saddened, if we regard them steadily, make the Gospel of Christ—the Son of God and the Son of man—intrinsically credible. Nothing less could meet our wants, and this does meet them. But, in order that we may gain the inspiration of the glad-tidings, we must strive at least to reach forward to its scope, strive to find how it passes on this side and that beyond the utmost range of human thought, how it covers the whole field of being in which it is revealed, how it encourages and sustains us in the endeavour to understand practically that we are all bound one to another in the turmoil of our present conflict, bound to the past of which we are the children, bound to the future of which we are the parents, in the fellowship of our manhood which Christ came to save. As long as we isolate ourselves, and strive to stand apart, peace is impossible. But joy comes—the joy of Christ which no one taketh away—when we are enabled to sympathise in deed and in truth with the purpose of His redeeming love, to apprehend, however feebly and imperfectly, that below the wastes and wearinesses and wickednesses, on which we look, enduring beyond all that is of time, subsisting beyond all that is of space, He is the Life in whom we live. *I came,* He said, *that they may have life and may have abundance* (John x. 10).

* * *

The essential relations of the Family introduce us at once to this vast, unseen, spiritual, eternal life to which every one of our lives is in its measure contributory and in which all find their unity and consummation.

* * *

The poorest mother who clasps her newborn infant to her breast has found, if but for a moment, the secret of life. To live for others, to suffer for others, is the inevitable condition of our being. To accept the condition gladly is to find it crowned with its own joy.

Other relations in the family emphasise in various ways this fundamental fact * * * helping us to feel that isolation is the measure of lasting pain, that we live truly exactly in proportion as we go out of ourselves and enter into the fulness of the experience of those whom we serve and by whom in turn we are served. Let anyone for instance, looking to his own home, put on one side the trivial commonplace occasions on which he has sacrificed others to himself, and on the other those in which he has sacrificed himself to others, and he will see that life is indeed the discipline of love, and that love is the soul of life.

* * * * Again, we have not only a domestic ancestry, and a domestic heritage. We have also a national ancestry and a national heritage. A great part of our lives is made up of that which we have every one received in common as Englishmen. And this splendid patrimony is not for display, not for pride, but for most laborious and solemn employment. Patriotism, like affection, may unhappily degenerate into selfishness; but it may by God's grace be the devout expression of a duty to humanity. It may be a trembling thanksgiving on the

part of those who feel that, as they have received much, much will be required of them. In any case the love of our country, the intense watchful interest in the growth or the waning of its influence, the passionate desire that it may be made a herald of righteousness and peace to the nations, does lie deep in the souls of all of us.

There is I most sadly know another side to the picture. There are bitter feuds of party, intrigues, seditions, wars, just as there are the jealousies, the quarrels, the estrangements of home. The greater body has its grievous sicknesses, its fevers and its frenzies, even as the less. But the ocean lies deep and still below the storms which trouble its surface. The life, the natural life, is more than its corruptions: more for each one of us, I trust, in actual enjoyment: more assuredly in its promises of hope. For is there one among us who has not known again and again in the last few years the throbbings of this larger life, as his own, when he has waited day after day for tidings of the little army which entered without power of return upon untravelled passes to relieve a beleaguered city, when he has heard of the silent night march of untried troops which made the end of a doubtful struggle possible, when he has found that statesmen could dare to consider the claims of justice in a moment of disaster, when he has entered into the fulness of a royal sorrow? Is there one of us who has not known that this life is fuller, deeper, intenser than his private pleasures and cares. Is there one of us who has not known that the tidings which meet us at such crises are more than the materials of passing excitement, that they call into vital energy the potency of the sympathy within us, through which we grow conscious that as a people we are one.

* * *

Thus the life of the family, the life of the nation, bear us far beyond the visible from which they start. Through those larger forms of life we enter on the unseen. We become prepared to understand at last that description of our position as Christians here on earth in which we read that *we are come*—not that we shall come—*unto mount Zion and unto the city of the living God, the heavenly Jerusalem, and to innumerable hosts of angels, to the general assembly and church of the firstborn, who are enrolled in heaven, and to God the Judge of all, and to the spirits of just men made perfect, and to Jesus the Mediator of a new Covenant*...(Hebr. xii. 22 ff.). We learn to acknowledge that these words, glorious as they are, reaching far beyond all that we can think or feel, are written for us; that that fellowship with men and angels and God is for us; for us, not at some indefinite future but now, now when we stand like the Hebrews of old, to whom the words were first addressed, in the midst of sore temptations, on the verge of changes which we are unable to anticipate.

* * *

Such ideas of a boundless life reaching from the visible to the invisible, in which we all share, may seem to many to be strange, and visionary and difficult. I should not offer them now as the foundation of all I have to say here, if I did not believe them to be at present of momentous practical importance : if I did not find in them myself, as I said before, the solution of the enigmas of life which our age proposes to us. The pitiless sphinx—if I may recal the familiar story—sets before each generation the old riddle in a new shape; and the answer is still always, man in some new form. This is the answer which we have to make good and if by the Spirit's guidance we can read its meaning : if we can win for ourselves—for it must be a work of labour and discipline—the conviction of the reality of that human life which is made known in Christ, in His suffering and in His triumph : if we can realise that we all are members one of another, members of one body shaped in its unity through all time; then hope rises before us as great as our heart.

For the life, the whole life, belongs equally to every part. All that lives, lives with the one life. If we know that we share in this we can wait for the revelation of its action. Meanwhile every true human joy is ours; every true human sorrow is ours; every brother's weakness and sin is ours also. Sympathy in affliction is the pledge of sympathy in triumph. *If we suffer with Christ we shall also reign with Him*, sharing His sovereignty over a renovated earth.

There is much, very much, in the circumstances of life which requires readjustment; but as we believe in the one life in Christ we shall not attempt to deal directly with symptoms and achieve superficial reforms. We shall seek to overcome the disease by quickening the healthy energy of the vital forces. To this end we can all contribute. In this labour we are all called to be fellow-workers with God. What the issue may be we are not careful to prejudge. But we are sure that the spiritual life of a people will find an outward form corresponding to its power and to its beauty.

> For of the soul the body form doth take:
> For soul is form and doth the body make.

* * *

For this life, shadowed forth in the life of the Family, the Nation, the Church, we were made; for this vast, unseen, spiritual, eternal life, a life growing with our growth and widening with our widening thoughts. The sense of such a life restores a real harmony to the facts of the world. It brings the power of the Incarnation and of the Resurrection of Christ near to each one of us. It supplies a motive sufficient to kindle our enthusiasm and consume our selfishness. It is more real, more abiding, more potent, than the shadows which we seem to be and the shadows which we commonly pursue.

* * *

A man's life is not in his abundance, no, not in the idle overflow of hoarded treasure: a man's life is *not from that which he pursueth*, no, not from the natural gifts of fortune or rank or intellect; but from the use of every gift which love makes for the service of God in Whom we are and Who is in us.

* * *

Such appear to be some of the lessons which the Abbey brings home to us: such is the spirit in which I have endeavoured to interpret them. May others be enabled to enforce them with unmeasurably greater power and truer insight. *Behold, the Judge standeth before the doors.*

Those who are familiar with recent theories of Social Morality will recognise how much I owe to two writers who are not often joined together in an acknowledgment of deep gratitude, Comte and Maurice. In the summer of 1867 I was able to analyse carefully the *Politique Positive,* and I found in it a powerful expression of many salient features of that which I had long held to be the true social embodiment of the Gospel, of a social ideal which the faith in Christ is alone, I believe, able to realise. Two years later I read Maurice's *Social Morality*. Few books can teach nobler lessons; and I should find it hard to say how much I owe to it directly and by suggestion.

In the endeavour to realise the social condition of Europe at the time of the rise of the Franciscans

I found great help from Mr Brewer's masterly introduction to the *Monumenta Franciscana*[1], and from F. Laurent's *Etudes sur l'histoire de l'humanité. La Féodalité et l'Église,* 1861.

The remains of Francis himself are collected in a most convenient form in the edition of Von der Burg (1849). The references are made to this edition.

In the general account of the Society of Friends I owe much to T. Clarkson's *Portraiture of Quakerism* (1806); and also to Canon Curteis' wise and sympathetic estimate of the work of the Quakers in his *Bampton Lectures: Dissent in relation to the Church of England* (1872).

The references to Fox's *Journal* are made to the seventh edition (London, 1852).

B. F. W.

CAMBRIDGE,
April 22, 1887.

[1] An examination of Dugdale will shew that Mr Brewer greatly underrates the importance of the later Franciscan buildings in England. Their buildings at Cambridge 'were not only an ornament and grace, but had great conveniences for holding the assemblies and doing all the business of the University' (Ascham ap. Dugdale *Monasticon*, vi. 1509). At Oxford 'their buildings were...stately and magnificent...not to be equalled with other in Oxon, either college or convent, except St Frideswide's and Ousney...' (Ant. Wood, *id.* p. 1530).

NOTICE TO THE SECOND EDITION.

THE generous welcome which this little book has received from critics and correspondents is in itself a sufficient proof, if any proof be needed, of the deep interest which is felt far and wide in the Social teaching of the Gospel. It cannot be proclaimed too often that the Christian Life is the proper evidence of the Christian Faith. Our strength lies in fellowship with a Living God Who speaks to us now as clearly as He spoke in the first age, and offers us the support which we require for the work of to-day. The truest reverence for the past is that which regards its glories as the pledge of a nobler future; and the generation to whom we commit our hopes will, I cannot doubt, realise them.

ΚΑΙ ΤΟ ΠΝΕΥΜΑ ΚΑΙ Η ΝΥΜΦΗ ΛΕΓΟΥϹΙΝ ΕΡΧΟΥ· ΚΑΙ Ο ΑΚΟΥΩΝ ΕΙΠΑΤΩ ΕΡΧΟΥ· ΚΑΙ Ο ΔΙΨΩΝ ΕΡΧΕϹΘΩ, Ο ΘΕΛΩΝ ΛΑΒΕΤΩ ΥΔΩΡ ΖΩΗϹ ΔΩΡΕΑΝ.

B. F. W.

WESTMINSTER,
Aug. 28, 1888.

I.

CHRISTIAN ASPECTS OF THE ELEMENTS OF SOCIAL LIFE.

I. *The Foundation.*

II. *The Family.*

III. *The Nation.*

II.

CHRISTIAN ASPECTS OF THE ORGANISATION OF SOCIAL LIFE.

I. *The Kingdom of God.*

II. *Mediæval Efforts: the Franciscans.*

III. *Modern Efforts: the Quakers.*

IV. *Present Problems.*

APPENDIX.

Types of Apostolic Service.

I.

CHRISTIAN ASPECTS OF THE ELEMENTS OF SOCIAL LIFE.

I. *The Foundation.*

II. *The Family.*

III. *The Nation.*

IV. *The Race.*

V. *The Church.*

Other foundation can no man lay than that which is laid, even Jesus Christ.

1 Cor. iii. 11.

I. *THE FOUNDATION.*

IT is my purpose on the four following Sun- 1.
days to carry a little further into detail the thoughts which have occupied us on the last two seasons of our meeting here. We saw then how the Epistle to the Hebrews met difficulties not unlike our own when they first came upon the apostolic Church, by offering new views of the Person of Christ. We saw how the fact of the Incarnation, under various aspects, satisfies and transcends the loftiest aspirations and the largest hopes of men. I wish now to ask you to consider with me how our faith in the historic Gospel, in Christ, Born, Crucified, Ascended, guides, supports, encourages us in dealing with problems of social life.

I propose then to consider in succession the Christian conceptions of the Family, the Nation, the Race, the Church; but before doing this I desire this afternoon to define the foundation on which our social fabric must rest. I desire to shew how the Apostle's words are literally true for

I. us, true in their apparent exclusiveness, true in their real universality: *other foundation can no man lay than that which is laid, even Jesus Christ.*

I need not dwell on the importance, nay the necessity, of the inquiry which I have indicated. It is forced upon us by the currents of modern thought. On every side imperious voices trouble the repose which our indolence would wish to keep undisturbed. We can no longer dwell apart in secure isolation. The main interests of men are once again passing through a great change. They are most surely turning from the individual to the society. And if as Christians we are too often engrossed by disputes on points which seem to be for the most part either beneath or beyond the scope of our noblest powers, others are finding expression for inarticulate cries which come from the very centre of our common life. This being so, I do not think that our real controversies in the immediate future are likely to be speculative: they threaten to be terribly practical. Behind the disputes of words, the abstract reasonings about the Being of God or the constitution of man, which occupy a large place even in popular literature, lie the fundamental questionings of social duty: What is the basis and measure of our mutual obligations? What is the source of our weakness and of our strength? What is or ought to be our aim, our ideal, as men living human lives? What, in other words, is the foundation on which a kingdom of God can be built, and how can we do our part in hastening its establishment? I.

The answers to such questions as these are, I believe, to be found—to be found only as they always have been found since the first age—in the Christian life answering to the Christian Faith. But, I repeat, they are to be found. They are not permanent and uniform. They are not ready for our use without effort. They must be sought for, shaped, realised. They must answer to our time, our education, our place in the order of the world. The knowledge out of which they will spring must be immediate, direct, personal, if it is to be vital and availing. We must go back to the very source of Divine energy for the inspiration which we need, if we are to make healthy progress and fulfil our office in the economy of God. We must not, as heirs of the past, rest complacently upon the treasures which we have received: we must by the help of our inheritance look further and deeper into the Divine mysteries than those who have gone before us, that we may in our turn add something to the wealth of our children.

And if it be said that the problems which the coming generation will have to face, problems of wealth and poverty, of luxury and want, of capital

I. and labour, of population, of class, of national responsibility, of peace and war, are to be solved irrespectively of the Faith, I can only reply that if I am a Christian I must bring every interest and every difficulty of man within the range of my religion: that I must believe that as it is Divine so it is inexhaustible: that I must proclaim at all cost—bearing sentence, as I shall do, against my own inconsistency and unbelief—that its supremacy extends to all social organisations, to all civil compacts, to all imperial designs, no less than to all doctrine of God and the single soul.

And if it be said again that the great ideas of Christianity have entered into popular opinion, that they have been so vitally assimilated by society, that we can dispense with further study of the facts by which they were suggested, I can only reply that the ideas of Christianity without the facts of Christianity offer a splendid vision which is shewn to be unattainable. The ideas of Christianity require the fact of a living Christ for their fulfilment. *Other foundation can no man lay than that which is laid, even Jesus Christ.* Christ Himself, the living Christ—Son of man and Son of God—alone presents to us, as we have seen on other occasions, the union of the seen and the unseen, of the finite and the infinite, of earth and heaven: the Lord Jesus Christ substitutes for the

world fleeting and unstable a present kingdom of I.
God: He communicates to that which is temporal, what nothing else can do, the spirit of an indissoluble life: He gives us, if we will open our hearts, a motive strong beyond all indifference, a power prevailing over all sin, a fulness of life victorious over all change.

And when I speak of this boundless efficacy of the Person of the living Christ, I do not speak of those subtle mysteries in the investigation of which the mind of man is soon wearied and baffled, but of that most Divine, most human Figure whom the heart recognises in the Gospels, of those central facts in which the Saviour of the world stands revealed to us once for all in the history of the race. We feel at once and we acknowledge His sovereign authority in general terms, but we are slow to interpret His message. When we look to His Birth, and Death and Resurrection, are we not constrained to confess sadly that we have in Him a revelation which has not yet found that social expression which sooner or later it must find? For the Christian view of life, answering to the Christian view of the Person of Christ, must be distinguished from every view of life which leaves out Christ. As Christians we are not left as other men to quicken our impulses by noble abstractions or splendid

I. guesses. As Christians we are not constrained as other men to acquiesce in the presence of unconquerable suffering. As Christians we are not condemned as other men to gazé with stern resignation upon the spectacle of lost good.

If the Word became flesh, the brotherhood of men is a reality for us.

If the Son of God was crucified, the fall, and with it the redemption, are realities for us.

If the Son of man rose again from the dead, the eternal significance of our short space of labour is a reality for us.

Yes: the Person of Christ—made known in His Nature and His Work—gives to us in these three great regions of practical thought historical certainties which answer to the manifold instincts, experiences, imaginings of all ages. Christ sets before us in Himself, in what He has done and is, a final revelation of the relation of man to man, of the actual condition of humanity, of the destiny of life. When we fix our eyes steadily upon Him we see that our conceptions of society, of morality, of providence reflect light from His Image. We see that all men are brethren: that all men are fallen: that all men are made in the Divine counsel to gain the likeness of God through the completest development of their earthly powers. By this revelation we recognise that Jesus Christ

is indeed the Foundation of every human fellow- I.
ship. And on us therefore the duty is laid of confessing Christ, if we believe on Him, of shewing openly to the world that our one Foundation is able to support the fabric which answers to the present needs of society, that it marks out lines of enduring effort, that it gives unity to the varied strivings of all who are looking towards the dawn.

In the Birth, the Death, the Resurrection of Christ we see, I repeat, the brotherhood, the fall, the destiny of men; and by these three words we are directed to three social lessons of the Person of Christ which, as it appears to me, we still require to learn.

1. In Christ all men are brethren. The phrase has become a commonplace before its meaning has been grasped. For our relationship one to another does not depend on any remote descent: it is not perilled by any possible discovery as to the origin or the antiquity of man: it is not bound by the conditions of the outward life: it is not measured by the course of days and years: it is not closed by death. The brotherhood of men seen in Christ is a question not of genealogy but of being. It rests upon the present and abiding fatherhood of God, Who in His Son has taken our common nature to Himself. We may acknowledge this God-made kinsmanship, or we may

I. neglect it; but none the less we all are not only brethren in constitution, brethren in death, but brethren in Christ, brethren for evermore.

Such a conception of human brotherhood is widely different from the conceptions which men have framed for themselves out of connexions of blood or interest, of contiguity or feeling. And if we can once grasp it through the teaching of the Holy Spirit, it cannot be inoperative. Such a conception transforms not the conditions but the meaning of life. It stirs us to spread the power of a spiritual civilisation, for it is our own cause: it supports us in personal failure, for others supply our wants. It prepares the perception of a harmony between man and the world by emphasising
Gen. i. 27. the Divine element in man made in the image of the Creator. According as its influence prevails all life becomes an energy of fellowship, of fellowship with God, and of fellowship with men in God, with men not as chosen by any capricious or personal rule, but with men simply as men. In this way the spirit of brotherhood quickens the spirit of sonship. The love which goes out from us comes back to us multiplied a thousandfold. As we rejoice to acknowledge one towards the other an irredeemable debt of service, our strength will grow to meet each fuller acknowledgement of duty. As we rejoice

to bring up the thought of Him who *is not ashamed* I.
to call us brethren in our intercourse with those Hebr. ii. 11.
most unlike ourselves, our vision of life will be widened. As we rejoice to follow Him, even through the desolations of sin and selfishness, we shall draw light and warmth from His glorious Presence, though our own vision is clouded and our own hearts grow chill.

Bitter experience teaches us how grievously we need the help of this thought of brotherhood, of the brotherhood of brethren in Christ. We can all see in the retrospect of our lives—in the retrospect of the last year or of the last week—what hasty judgments, what ungenerous words, what ill-advised plans, would have been avoided if we could have realised at the crisis of decision the eternal bond which underlies our personal differences; if we could have looked forward to the eternal issues which flow from the circumstances of our ordinary intercourse. We can all see with what access of devotion we should have laboured for the fallen, for the ignorant, for the absent, if we had regarded them in the moments of our depression or weariness as children of our Father, inseparable from ourselves. We can all see how our prayers and confessions and thanksgivings would have gained in intensity and meaning if we had

I. felt that the daily record of human sorrows and crimes and labours is not merely a satisfaction of idle curiosity but a revelation of the movement of a life which reaches every one of us in its glory and in its shame. In that case an energy of infinite power would have been kindled by the light of infinite trust.

2. All men are brethren in Christ. That is the first principle of the interpretation of life which comes from the thought of Christ's Person. And next in the Death of Christ we have a revelation of the Fall. The sense of this truth is, I will venture to say, a condition of hope. No view of the human state is so inexpressibly sad as that which leaves out the Fall. The existence of evil in its many forms, as self-will, and suffering and vice and crime, cannot be gainsaid; and, if this evil belongs to the essence of man as created, then there can be no prospect of relief here or hereafter. Sin will propagate sin in inevitable succession, as the greatest of ancient poets sang. Misery will be as the shadow which man casts when the sun is brightest. There can be nothing in him to drive out that which is part of his true self. The stream as it flows will always fall below its source. And this awful and inexorable rule knows in nature no reversal or repeal. Endless retribution is the plain teaching of that in-

variable sequence which we call natural law. I.
Effectual forgiveness is the revelation of the Gospel. And this mystery of forgiveness is unveiled to us, as far as our sight can look upon it, in the fact of a Redemption answering to the fact of a Fall, in death endured and death overcome. For the rest it is enough for us to know that an enemy hath done this which covers the earth with gloom, and that One stronger than he hath spoiled him. It is enough for us to know that evil is foreign and intrusive and therefore conquerable. The strength for the conflict in the midst of which we find ourselves comes to us from without, from the Spirit of the Son of man, and therefore we can prevail in spite of our own weakness. The ambitious restlessness of merit is banished for ever. In its place comes the confident humility of faith.

I do not say that all the darkness of sin and suffering is removed by the glory which flows from the Cross of Christ. But I do say that light is given us there sufficient for our journey: that power is given us sufficient for our work: that as our perception of the darkness over the earth grows keener we are moved by the spectacle of the Cross to look with intenser confidence for the help which in the end cannot fail, and to rest with a more complete submission in that will of Love

I. which denies to us the vision of an accomplished triumph.

3. There is yet a third characteristic by which the view of life referred to the Person of Christ differs from all other views. The Resurrection teaches us that in Christ man is not immortal only but incorruptible: that all that belongs to the fulness of his nature, all that answers to his continuous growth, all that he gathers round him from day to day in habit and action, all that goes to make up that mysterious sum of powers, senses, passions, feelings, limitations, which he calls his body, is part of what shall be. And, if the former points on which I have touched, the social lessons of Christ's Birth and Death, mark new relations in Christ of man to his fellow-men and of man to God, this lesson of Christ's Resurrection marks, so to speak, a new relation of man to self. It shews us how we are shaping slowly out of things transitory that which will abide for ever: that death will not separate from us that which is of the earth but will invest that which before was of the earth with incorruption, or rather will reveal it as being what it is, eternal; that, in the words of St Paul, when we put off
2 Cor. v. 4. mortality we shall be *not unclothed but clothed upon.*

This thought is, as we must feel at once, of overwhelming solemnity. There is no need to develop it in words. It would indeed be intolerable if the believer were not *in Christ.* But as it is, we can take it with its tremendous consequences for our protection and for our encouragement: for our protection when temptation comes to us with fair promises of future impunity: for our encouragement when disappointment closes over the unfruitful toil on which we have lavished our best efforts. I.

To sum up, then, these three thoughts, men are brethren, men are fallen and redeemed, men are incorruptible, stand out before us in the Birth and Death and Resurrection of Christ as a solid foundation for the Christian fabric of life. They are in their application absolute and universal. They are confirmed and brought home to us in various ways in the ordinances of the Church. If we contemplate them calmly and patiently, in themselves and in the facts by which they are revealed, we shall find that they reach through our whole being: that they lay open counsels of God which extend beyond the believer and the Church to the whole world: that they must mingle with every speculation and colour every purpose of the Christian. But they must be taken as the basis of our social scheme, and not as an appendage to it. We cannot bring them at pleasure to crown an edifice which we have reared independently. Let us

I. however only believe the simple message of the Gospel, the plain utterances of our baptismal Creed, or pray with faltering lips for grace to believe them, and we shall know that for the noblest hopes of men, for the fairest constructions of wisdom, for the enduring fabric of society *none other foundation can be laid than that which is laid, even Jesus Christ.*

The foundation is laid, laid once for all, and we wait for the glorious consummation when the Lord shall complete what He has begun. Mean-
Phil. iii. 13 f. while it is our part, as we still look to Him, to strive towards the end, to strive as those who have learnt what is the goal of labour: to strive as those who are assured that in each one lies the
2 Pet. iii. 12. power of hastening the coming of the Saviour: to strive as those who have found the key to the
1 John ii. 2. great enigma of life, looking on all men as sharers with us of a nature which Christ has raised to heaven: looking on sin as that which only the
John i. 29. Son of God could take away by taking it to Him-
1 Cor. xv. 42. self: looking on the little duties and cares of each passing day as the elements out of which we are building an illimitable future; looking, in a word, to Christ Born, Crucified, Ascended, as to Him in whom is the promise and the power of unity, redemption, perfection which answer to the utmost wants of man and of the world.

II.

THE FAMILY.

I bow my knees unto the Father, from Whom every Family in heaven and on earth is named.

EPH. iii. 14, 15.

THE FAMILY.

WHEN we reflect upon the circumstances of II.
our life we are at once met by two facts which at first sight appear to be irreconcileable. We feel at each moment that we are responsible, responsible for the past which we recal and for the future to which we look forward. And at the same time we recognise that we are dependent on our descent and on our environment, limited both in action and in thought by laws which we cannot evade. Further reflection opens the vision of an underlying harmony between these conflicting experiences. We come to see that the completest conception which we can form of moral freedom is the willing fulfilment of the absolute law of our existence. He is free, he alone is free, who discerns the end and the method of his being, and follows with glad obedience the course which he finds marked out for him. And as Christians we believe that this freedom has been again brought within the reach of fallen humanity by the Incarnation of the Word, in Whom the

II. relations of men to the world, to the race, to God, have been set before us with a moving power, made effectual to mould our lives by the grace of the Spirit Whom He has sent to us. (John xiv. 26; xvi. 13—15.)

Life then, Christian life, will be best guided according as we know best the conditions under which we are called to live. These conditions are indeed so many present lessons of God given to His children, and like all the lessons of God they have an infinite meaning. The son, as he grows, understands more and more of his Father's counsel. Each fragment of the great order in which we are placed brightens and grows more glorious as we study it; and, if we offer ourselves to the influence of that Divine teaching which is for the moment within our reach, we shall stand in a right attitude towards the undiscovered sum of heavenly mysteries by which we are surrounded on all sides.

Now when we inquire into the conditions of our life, one thing is obvious at once. We are not made to live alone. The existence of the world is a fact, a self-luminous fact, of which we must take account, no less than the existence of God and the existence of our own souls. Even our communion with God must be through the fulness of life. There may be times when hermit-isolation becomes a duty, as it may be a duty to cut off

the right hand or to pluck out the right eye, II.
but it exhibits a mutilation and not an ideal of life. All the anarchy and half the social errors by which we are troubled spring from placing the individual, the self, at the centre of all things. No view can be more flagrantly false. It is impossible to resolve the world into a multitude of isolated men. It is impossible to picture in imagination even one isolated man. A man who had grown up alone would not be a man. When we come into being we are sons. When we first begin to act we have been necessarily in some degree disciplined and educated. To the last what we have inherited immeasurably outweighs what we have acquired.

Man in a word is made by and made for fellowship. The Family and not the individual is the unit of mankind. This fact is the foundation of human life to which we must look for the broad lines of its harmonious structure. And we shall not look in vain. For the Family exhibits in the simplest and most unquestionable types the laws of dependence and trust, of authority and obedience, of obligation and helpfulness by which every form of true activity is regulated. The Family enables us to feel that the destination of all our labours, the crown of all our joys, the lightening of all our sorrows, the use of

II. all our endowments, is social. Under no other circumstances are the imperious personal instincts of our nature so happily brought into subjection as under those which the Family supplies. In the Family love makes service, as it ought to be, its own reward, and transforms suffering into gladness. In the Family, as has been nobly said, *living for others* becomes the strict corollary of the patent fact that we *live by others.* In the Family we learn to set aside the conception of right, and to place in its stead the conception of duty, which alone can give stable peace to peoples or to men. So it is that the popular estimate of the Family is an infallible criterion of the state of society. Heroes cannot save a country where the idea of the Family is degraded; and strong battalions are of no avail against homes guarded by faith and reverence and love. Classical history is a commentary on this truth. The national life of Greece lasted barely for three generations in spite of the undying glory of its literature and the unrivalled triumphs of its art, because there the Family fell from its proper place. A constitution and laws reared on a lofty estimate of the Family gave Rome the sovereignty of the world. And more than this: Roman legislation which was based on the Family institutions of the old Republic survived the dissolution of the

Empire, and after more than two thousand years II.
is still powerful in the civil courts of Europe.

The Family indeed is not only an expression of Divine law. It is, under the conditions of earth, in some sense a reflection of the Divine nature. Every Family, every Fatherhood, derives that in Eph. iii. 15 (Gk.)
virtue of which it is from the One Father. We must therefore strive with reverent patience to enter into the meaning of the Family if we desire to understand the Divine conditions of our life. As we do this we shall see that a perfect Family includes three primary relations, those of husband
and wife, of parent and child, of brothers and III
sisters. And these three relations reveal the essential laws of all human fellowship. They are, if I may be permitted to use the phrase, the original sacraments of Society. They reveal to us the inherent incompleteness of the individual life completed in a typical union: that is the idea of Marriage. They reveal to us the correlative responsibilities of government and devotion, hallowed by love: that is the idea of Fatherhood. They reveal to us the inalienable ties of a common nature in the direct connexion of blood: that is the idea of Brotherhood. But while the widest differences of position and duty coexist in the Family and find consecration within its circle, the whole Family is one, one in the

II. common heritage of shame and glory, one in the sympathetic response of all to the suffering and joy of every member.

1. The idea of Marriage, the basis of the Family, is, I have said, the typical completion of our individual incompleteness. Marriage is not simply a relation of contract, established to secure the orderly transmission of special rights in due succession, but the sacred fulfilment of life. Man or woman alone represents only half of the powers and capacities and feelings of humanity. And no real approach can be made to the consummation of our common nature by any attempt on the part of woman to cultivate those elements in it which are characteristic of man, or on the part of man to make his own that which is truly womanly. Such attempts only impoverish the race. Nothing less than the union of man and woman in their developed diversity gives us the image of a perfect human being, and raises our thoughts to a higher existence than that of our divided personalities. At the same time each of the natures thus joined together strengthens, elevates, purifies the other, not by the assertion of its own supremacy, not by the communication of its own peculiarities, but by the rendering of its appropriate service. The husband grows more manly, the wife grows more womanly, as they realise

each in the other the possession of that which II.
they severally need and yet cannot provide from within themselves.

As we dwell on these facts we come to perceive the meaning of the Lord's words when He said of the man and the wife, with a reference to creation which must as yet remain obscure, *the twain shall become one flesh.* *This is* in- Matt. xix. 5.
deed *a great mystery,* a great revelation, and Eph. v. 32.
with our present faculties we can master but little of it. Yet we can dimly feel whither it directs us. We can feel how Marriage by its necessary conditions provides for the extension of fellowship through the union of different Families. We can feel how this supreme relationship invests all the other relationships of life with a Divine solemnity. We can feel how it shews with eloquent distinctness that absolute trust is the condition of abiding fellowship and absolute self-surrender the condition of the highest influence. If trust be incomplete Marriage, we know, cannot have its perfect work. If trust be broken, Marriage perishes. But, by interchange of thought and hope and prayer, in Marriage trust ripens into faith. And that faith, carried out into the world, is the secret of the blessedness of life.

2. Marriage in a word is the Divine pattern

II. and ground of human communion, the original sacrament of completed manhood. But the Family has, as we have seen, other lessons; and though the ideas of authority and equality, of dependence and service are included in the relation of Marriage, it is in the other two relations of the Family, Fatherhood and Brotherhood, that we learn most fully how these universal principles are realised under the varying circumstances of age, rank, power, which are necessary for the continuance and for the unity of the social body. Fatherhood is, so to speak, the Divine pattern and ground of authority: Brotherhood the Divine pattern and ground of equality. And it is instructive to observe that while Marriage, as the supreme sign of faith, rests upon choice, these are in their essence independent of it. The son is placed in a position of subjection: the brother is placed in a position of obligation, without the least power of avoiding the consequences which these positions involve. We may for various reasons withhold the confession of love by which we seek outside ourselves for the abiding completion of our own imperfect nature; but we cannot, while the world lasts, take out of it that which claims our obedience or that which claims our help. These relations of reverence and service are founded not upon choice but in nature. And if once we study

them as they are offered for our daily contempla- II.
tion in the Family, we shall be delivered from the wild strivings of rebellious selfishness in society at large, whether it is turned by the few into tyranny or by the many into lawlessness.

Fatherhood is, I have said, the pattern, or, to repeat the phrase which I have used before, the original sacrament of authority: sonship, of reverence and obedience. The necessity of the relation lies in the harmony of our constitution. If it were not so, and we must face the alternative, order could only be maintained by selfish fear or by no less selfish hope. But in a Family, even the rudest and simplest, there is, we know, something different from force which gives weight to the parent's voice: something different from terror which inspires the child's answer. The relation of parent and child carries with it that which no external power can create and which no external power can destroy. There is in the very order of things a subtle influence which gives to authority its responsible privilege and to obedience its tender dignity. And this truth of the eternal majesty of authority, of the eternal loveliness of reverent obedience, commended to us still in our childhood, is not the least precious part of our social heritage as Englishmen. It has hitherto been hallowed and guarded in our homes; and

II. if we take it into our hearts consciously, gladly, thoughtfully, as it is open before our eyes, we shall soon discover how it interprets other relations of life which can be regarded in their true aspect only in the light of Fatherhood.

For the lesson of Fatherhood passes at once within the Family to the connexion of masters and servants, which cannot with impunity be degraded into a mere bargain, and which may be ennobled by real sympathy. It passes on without to the connexion of employer and workman, which ceases, I cannot but say, to be human if it is made to mean only so much labour for so much money. It passes to the connexion of owner and occupier which cannot be stable, if an inherited right is supposed to dispense with present duties. It passes to the connexion of government and citizen, which is simply a compact of limited slavery, unless we recognise above us that which we may modify but which we cannot make, a manifestation of eternal authority which we are born to treat with loyal reverence.

3. There is still a third essential relation of the Family to be noticed, Brotherhood, the pattern, the original sacrament of equality. But this Divine equality is, as we have already seen, widely different from that external equality which men have looked for in some reconstruction of the

world. It is inherent and permanent: it is mani- II.
fested in variety: it is consummated in sacrifice. The ties of blood may be dissembled, disregarded, disgraced, but they cannot be destroyed. 'Brothers are brothers evermore.' The differences of character and ability which are found in a Family furnish, in the happy experience of all of us, rich materials which a common love consecrates to the service of all. The sense of equality which home blesses is most perfect, not when we make the claim to receive the payment of a debt owed, but when we feel the power to pay a debt acknowledged.

As brothers and sisters we can learn this lesson of divine Brotherhood, learn it by a teaching ever present and absolutely unimpeachable, and the lesson will remain with us for our comfort when we go out into wider fields of activity. Just as the idea of Fatherhood hallows the conditions of inequality which belong to the surface of life, seen in the movement of succession, so this idea of Brotherhood reveals to us the great depths of our being in which we are all equal. It enables us to claim and to realise a fellowship with those who are separated from us. It gives hope under the consciousness of the fragmentariness of our individual work. It keeps fresh the generous impulses which bind kinsmen together

II. though scattered through distant lands. It tends to counteract that spirit of isolating competition which is eating away the old repose and nobility of English life. It helps us to rise slowly towards the conception of a common humanity, called into existence by one Father, redeemed by one Incarnate Saviour, quickened by one infinite Spirit.

4. The constitution of the Family illuminates the social relations of men; and the life of the Family illuminates the meaning and the use of property. In the earliest ordering of the Family all the resources of the household were absolutely at the disposal of the head: wife and child were 'in his hand.' Even now the father practically controls, either by right or by natural influence, the disposal of the common store. But he dispenses it, so far as he obeys the common voice of mankind, not arbitrarily, still less for personal ends, but as the trustee for those who are bound to him. His wealth, in means, in leisure, in power, is the measure of his responsibility. He provides, not by benevolence but by duty, for the education, for the adequate development of the character and endowments, of all who are dependent on him: he guards them, as far as he can do, from the unforeseen consequences of the failure of health or strength. The fulfilment of these obligations is required by

his position, and it crowns his authority with blessing. It reveals to us how the concentration of riches, material or spiritual, becomes a social good, fruitful beyond any equality of possession. And it is obvious that the principle has a wider application, through which we may yet hope to see the varieties of external circumstances harmonised in the fulness of one life. II.

For this cause, then, even that we have received the knowledge of the great counsel of God and been called to work in His Church, of which the Family is the type and sacrament, we *bow* our *knees unto the Father from Whom every Family in heaven and earth is named*, that He would shew us His will more clearly from day to day, and give us strength to fulfil it. For those who have followed me so far will acknowledge, I trust, that they have actually about them in their Families a revelation of God in which they can find the principles at least of the right answers to many of the most urgent problems of society: they will acknowledge that the loftiest aspirations and the most difficult labours have in the home hearth that which may kindle them with a holier glow and direct them with a steadier light: they will acknowledge sadly—so at least I must acknowledge—that these open mysteries of the Family are too often unhonoured, unread,

II. unheeded: they will acknowledge that where discipline is most attractive we all seek rather to be ministered unto than to minister: that selfishness troubles and stains the very spring of sacrifice.

But, thanks be to God, the teaching of the Family is still left to us in England, rich in gracious lessons of authority and reverence and service. The ties of the Family are still held sacred by popular sentiment. So may we study them, while there is yet time, study them in the light of God's presence, and we shall need no other school of social duty. May we by the Spirit's help labour to fulfil them, and we shall need no other preparation for the greater offices of life, no other pledge that for these also the *Father from Whom every Family in heaven and earth is named* will give us the strength which we need.

III.

THE NATION.

The nations shall walk amidst the light [of the city of God] and the kings of the earth do bring their glory into it.

Apoc. xxi. 24.

THE NATION.

IT was my object last Sunday, to point out III. that the family and not the individual is the true unit of society: that the essential relations of the family—marriage, fatherhood, brotherhood—furnish us with the divine conceptions of fellowship, authority, equality which rule and animate the harmonious structure of human life: that they are in a true sense the original sacraments of humanity through which we can recognise and receive the blessings of the divine counsel: that we must study them with reverent patience, and yield ourselves to their influence with glad devotion, if we desire to fulfil our part in larger fields of action, when we are called to enter them.

For life cannot be completed within the sheltered precincts of the home. As the years go on the child enters naturally into a wider sphere. The friendships of school, the intercourse of business, reveal to the growing boy new obligations, new joys, new temptations, new conflicts, through which the lessons of earlier discipline

III. are extended and applied. He is constrained in a sense which he has not realised before to stand alone. He passes from the rule of love to the rule of law. The fact of his personal responsibility is pressed upon him by the administration of impartial and stern justice. He learns to be one of many, and in a varied companionship to give definiteness to that which he has in common with his fellows. In this way the idea of the nation, the society of neighbours, is called into active exercise to supplement the idea of the family, the society of kinsmen in blood. At the same time the life of the family is seen in its continuity and in its breadth in the life of the nation. Thus the nation is found to be the second type, the second broadening circle of social life.

I wish then this afternoon to mark some features in the nature and duties of national life. I wish to point out three things especially. I wish to point out that in this relation also we are bound one to another by ties which man did not invent and which man cannot destroy: that as citizens of a fatherland we have received an inheritance of blessings infinitely greater than any results obtainable by our own exertions: that we are constrained by every motive of thankfulness and justice to endeavour to realise, each in our own place, the great principles which should rule the administration of states, and to understand the circumstances which affect the special forms in which those principles ought to be and are embodied in our own country. III.

1. The idea of a nation is, I say, like the idea of the family, involved in the very constitution of man. It takes shape slowly—slowly in the individual and slowly in the race: it is profoundly influenced in its realisation by physical circumstances: its growth is hastened or retarded by external forces. But it does grow. The germ lies in the man—the son, the brother, the husband, the father. As soon as we begin to think we become conscious of objects beyond our private interests, which we pursue in common with our neighbours and by like methods. All attempts to explain the origin of states by a primitive contract between their members are idle fictions. All attempts to explain the continuance of states by the necessities of individual protection and convenience leave out of account the social instincts which are not less real, if at first they are less prevailing, than personal instincts. The generating, the sustaining, force of states is not material but spiritual. The soul at its noblest is the witness to its destiny. We are born and live, and we feel that we are

III. born and live, not for ourselves only, not for our families only, but for all about us. This being so the nation enables us to serve our neighbour, our brother in Christ, and to receive the benediction of his service. Language, law, government, religion, offer scope for the free action of the many and of the one. In these, truth, right, history, feeling, find step by step their permanent expression according to the experience of those who are moulded by the same forces in the same environment. Language, law, government, religion, are in fact the fruit and the proof of the life of the nation. They cannot be referred finally to the will or to the power of any individual. The poet and the legislator, the statesman and the evangelist, achieve their work by interpreting and not by creating thoughts in many hearts. The humblest human experience goes to form the oracle of the prophet. And, these four, if we will but listen to their voice—language, law, government, religion—remind us at every moment of a larger being in which we share and to which we may minister. They call us to strive in our turn to make the new thoughts and the new lessons, which are struggling for utterance through us, available, under happy
John iv. 38. conditions, for those who shall enter into our labours.

2. We are then, as citizens of a nation, debtors to an incalculable past. This, if often overlooked, is a fact which calls for reverent and thankful acknowledgment. We cannot if we would start afresh from our simple manhood. Our national characteristics surround us with an atmosphere equally subtle and pervading. What we are and what we can be has been in a large measure determined for us by our English ancestors. They have stored up for our ready use, by toil and thrift, by insight and love, material and spiritual treasures which no one generation could amass. They have fixed the standard of our language, not in the greatest of human poets, but in the Bible. They have handed down from generation to generation safeguards of independence and justice, sealed not unfrequently by suffering and martyrdom. They have united, imperfectly it may be as yet, but still they have united class to class by the sympathy of action and by the sense of responsibility. They have given to us, when the evils of age begin to make themselves felt, the vigour of fresh youth in the 'daughter-lands' of a new world. They have guarded with tender reverence for our inspiration a faith, of which this Abbey is a symbol, hospitable to all things true and honourable and just and pure and lovely and of good report, but III.

III. jealous that all shall be hallowed by His blessing through whom alone we come to the One Father.

They have, in a word, transmitted to us their life; and this life is the heritage not of a party, or of a class, but of all; and all have entered upon it. It is true that in ordinary circumstances we may not be able to measure the intensity of the common life which quickens us—how few ever notice the beating of their own hearts—but at rare intervals the words of a great writer, the advocacy of a great cause, the presence of a great trial, bring into view our vital fellowship, and we are allowed to see in its grandeur that which has never ceased to be active within us.

Two occasions, now in the distant past, rise before me still with unchangeable freshness, when every Englishman, I believe, rejoiced to know even through anxiety and sorrow that the nation was still one, one in the maintenance of law, one in the devotion of loyalty. Five and twenty years ago, when peace or war hung upon the answer to a claim made in the deliberate assertion of a legal right, the issue was awaited throughout the empire with calm resolution; and when the claim was yielded, not one expression of pride or selfishness marred the thanksgiving for a bloodless victory.

Again, at a later time, when it seemed that the succession of our royal line would be broken, the heart of the whole people was moved as the heart of one man, not for a son, or a husband, or a father only, but for a prince, who was felt to represent to his people something far more than personal qualities, and to bind us all, as no other could do, to a glorious past. That memorable season of suspense and deliverance and grateful joy was, I cannot doubt, a crisis in the history of our monarchy; and when I think of it my thoughts go back not to the august ceremonial of a nation's thanksgiving at St Paul's, but to a plain white cross in the churchyard at Sandringham, on which are inscribed the words which tell the story of death and life—'*One is taken and another left,*'—the servant taken and remembered: the lord left and not unmindful of the awful presence in which he has been. Surely this most touching and open confession of equality reveals to us the secret of that III.

> Sober freedom, out of which there springs
> Our loyal passion for our temperate kings.

For such revelations of national life as these we may well thank God. They open out before us, if only for a moment, its magnificent realities. They enable us to reflect what age-long tributes of courage, of counsel, of suffering have gone to foster and support it. They teach us to understand with what splendid capacities of strength

III. and tenderness it endows us. They force us to resolve, as grace may be given us, to transmit that which we have ourselves received purified and enriched to our children.

3. That we may do so, we must, as I have said, ponder the laws and circumstances of national life. We must not only busy ourselves, as we are bound to do, with the little interests which surround us, but rise to the sight of the eternal purposes which they are designed to further. We must bear in mind in this more extended sphere of action the three principles which the family commends to us, the principles of communion, of authority, of equality; and not rest till we can be sure that we are swayed in our political judgments by their salutary influence.

For the nation no less than the family springs out of the acknowledgment of our personal incompleteness. As citizens we are all, high and low, rich and poor, dependent one on another. We need that is individually, for the fulness of our civic life, the peculiar gifts and offices of others to supply that which is wanting in ourselves. There could be no true nation, even as there could be no true family, without wide differences in power, in fortune, in duty, among those who compose it. And the aim of the Christian patriot will be not to obliterate these differences but to harmonise them in their ripe development by shewing that they can minister to the vigour of one life. He will strive not to confound class with class, but to bind all classes together in their characteristic distinctness by the consciousness of mutual service. He will set forth as his great aim the perfection of each part not for its own sake but as a contributory to the whole. He will labour to establish everywhere the central truth of morals, the central truth of faith, that man is stronger and more blessed through sacrifice than through self-assertion. He will seek to realise—last triumph of noble souls—that the brightest crown of action is the feeling of good done for which there is no reward. III.

> Paid by the world,—what dost thou owe
> Me? God might question: now instead,
> 'Tis God shall repay! I am safer so.

The nation again, no less than the family, is organised and controlled by an inherent authority. Through whatever instruments the authority may be administered, it is in itself not of man but of God. Authority is not created but recognised even in a successful revolution. Authority may be graced or obscured by the character of him who wields it, but essentially it can receive no glory and suffer no loss from man. St Peter

III. and St Paul, as we remember, honoured it in the tyrant Nero: Christ Himself acknowledged it in the selfish Pilate. There have been times when the sacredness of the divine ordinance has been transferred to the person of the sovereign; and now, on the other hand, we are tempted to derive the sanction of the authority itself from the character of the person who wields it. But it is possible to avoid the falsehood of both extremes. And the Christian patriot will keep the divine and human elements in the ruler separate in thought, while he prays ardently that they may be brought into the truest unison. He will know, and he will help others to know, that the stability of society is assured when we believe that its structure is not wholly of earth. He will rejoice to teach that reverence is the parent of self-respect and dignity. He will feel that the citizen who has learnt to look on government as the reflection, however incomplete, of an eternal order, has found the source of true nobility; for he who sees the Divine must himself be transfigured by it.

The nation, yet once more, no less than the family calls for the manifestation of a brotherhood, of an equality, that is, which is based upon the acknowledgment of a common nature. The realisation of such a brotherhood, such an equality,

among us is happily not yet beyond hope. The III.
power which is exercised by the mere words over the imagination of men shews that they are longing for the fact. And the fact of brotherhood, as we have seen, lies at the very foundation of our faith. It exists already wherever the Gospel finds a welcome, even if it be not shewn. The Christian patriot then will bend his energies to this above all things, that he may bring to light the social fellowship of his countrymen. He will not tire in urging others to confess in public, what home makes clear, that love and not interest is alone able to explain and to guide our conduct—love for something outside us, for something above us, for something more enduring than ourselves: that self-devotion and not self-assertion is the spring of enduring and beneficent influence: that each in his proper sphere—workman, capitalist, teacher—is equally a servant of the state, feeding in his measure that common life by which he lives: that work is not measured but made possible by the wages rendered to the doer: that the feeling of class is healthy, like the narrower affections of home, till it claims to be predominant: that we cannot dispense, except at the cost of national impoverishment, with the peculiar and independent services of numbers and of wealth and of thought, which respectively embody and

III. interpret the present, the past, and the future: that we cannot isolate ourselves as citizens any more than as men, and that if we willingly offer to our country what we have, we shall in turn share in the rich fulness of the life of all.

Such thoughts as these may appear to some to be vague and unpractical, far removed from the actual controversies and distresses of society. But if so, then the Gospel itself has no social meaning and no social power; and we must lay aside the sustaining hope that *the kings of the earth* shall *bring their glory into the city of God.* But I cannot accept for one moment this confession of
Matt. xi. 3. despair. I cannot *look for another* when the Presence of the Risen Christ is revealed over the world. Nay, rather, such thoughts as I have endeavoured to suggest, such thoughts alone, I believe, make our controversies endurable by thoughtful men and prepare relief for our distresses. It cannot but be that conflicts of party politics should continue. It cannot but be that we should find ourselves busily engrossed in details. It cannot but be that our souls should be wounded by griefs which as yet we cannot remove. For this very reason it is well that we should look from time to time to the foundation and issues, to the nature and sanctions, of a nation's life and a nation's work as seen through the teachings of

our faith. In that lofty prospect all Christians III. will recognise the one divine if distant goal of all their efforts. And they will carry away from the view on which their eyes have rested a sense of unity which will not be lost even in the struggles which must follow: a sense of dignity in honest service when they are busied with the simplest offices of duty: a sense of confident trust when the laws of God require men still to see the world, for which Christ died, darkened by sorrows for which they can find no remedy.

Yes: the vision of the Apocalypse is for us also. Beyond these crowded thoroughfares which bewilder us, these crushing palaces of commerce which overwhelm us, this sordid glare which dazzles and saddens us, rises before the believer the holy city, pure and still. There is no Temple there—that is, the symbol at once of religious fellowship and religious separation—for *the Lord God Almighty is the Temple thereof and the Lamb.* That Divine dwelling-place has no need of the sun—that is the symbol of the quickening energy of nature and the measure of time—for *the glory of God lightens it, and the lamp thereof is the Lamb. And the nations walk amidst the light thereof, and the kings of the earth do bring their glory into it;* offering, that is, each their peculiar

III. treasures, to fill up the manifested sovereignty of the Lord.

That is the end. Meanwhile till the end comes, and that the end may come, we must all so labour that our own nation may be enabled to bring her gift made fit for the Master's Presence through the harmonious ministry of every class and of every citizen.

IV.

THE RACE.

[God] made of one every nation of men for to dwell on all the face of the earth, having determined their appointed seasons and the bounds of their habitation that they should seek God....

Acts xvii. 26 f.

THE RACE.

THE relations of the Family school us, as we have seen, for our duties in the Nation. IV.
Trained by the happy discipline of our homes to feel the need of fellowship, the grace of authority, the joy of service, we soon recognise the divine lineaments of the state. We perceive naturally how the life of this larger body is sustained and purified and ennobled by the forces which are first revealed in Marriage, in Fatherhood, in Brotherhood. We gladly acknowledge that the forms of political order are something more than convenient provisions for the satisfaction of material needs. We find that we are truer men, truer Christians, in proportion as we recognise that the Nation is for the loyal citizen a revelation, blurred and mutilated it may be, but still a revelation of the original will of God, in behalf of the being whom He made in His own image to reach, through the natural processes of a life sustained by communion with Him, to His likeness.

IV. But we cannot rest here. As the teaching of the Family leads us to the idea of the Nation, so the teaching of the Nation leads us while the ages go forward, to the idea of the Race. While the ages go forward: for the old Roman had but one word for stranger and enemy. The Greeks sharply separated from themselves all other peoples as essentially inferior. The Hebrews alone of ancient peoples, in this respect true children of Abraham though in others the most exclusive of all, provided from the first for the admission of strangers to a full share in their most sacred privileges. But none the less the experience of life gradually leads men towards a larger communion. The sense of national friendships is slowly established between peoples not unequally matched; and still more slowly the strong are inspired with regard for the rights of the weak. In this way, little by little, the nations are brought to realise that there is in the order of the world a sacred fellowship between them as members of one Race: that what is true of the intercourse and duties of class and class, of party and party, in any single realm, is true of the mutual intercourse and duties of peoples, as elements of one humanity; that it may be in this greatest organisation of men, as in our own frames, that the parts which seem to be least and

1 Cor. xii. 22 ff.

weakest claim most abundant care. And these lessons lie at the very heart of the Gospel in which our one Creator is revealed to us as our one Redeemer, the Heir of all things. IV. Heb. i. 2.

Some, perhaps, may think that we can already discern the dawning of a new order which answers to the perception of a fuller truth. A large view of history encourages the belief. The progress in the old world from the Family through the many nations to the universal Empire seems to foreshadow the normal course of society. And in the new world, in spite of grave disturbing causes, we can notice how the Christian Faith first purified and confirmed the relations of the Family: then the relations of the state: and now is leading us by many signs to acknowledge the supremacy of wider ties.

But however this may be, though the lessons are, I have said, slowly learnt, the special circumstances of our own time have pressed them forward with unusual force. The increased facilities for the interchange of thought: the frequency of foreign travel: the development of commerce: have made the narrownesses and intolerances which were almost habitual in the last century no longer possible. We cannot for a moment forget that we are but one nation among many nations, who are our rivals in power and glory, distinct from us

IV. in character and institutions and history, and yet not alien from us as children of one Father on earth and in heaven.

But the recognition of this fellowship of nations is not without danger. We cannot but find it hard to reconcile a just sense of the great things which God has wrought for us with a like respect for His dealings with others. We are tempted to surrender one feeling or the other or both. We are tempted, that is, by the spirit of domination, by the spirit of imitation, and by the spirit of affected indifference; and these three spirits must be effectually exorcised before we can serve our Race or indeed have any true sense of its vital unity.

To us perhaps the spirit of domination is peculiarly perilous from the force of individuality in the English nature and from the conditions of our island home. Our first impulse is to claim universal supremacy for our own customs and opinions and forms of government: to regard each variation from our own standards of thought and action as the result of ignorance or degeneracy: to urge the adoption of our social institutions as the remedy for evils in other lands: to press patriotism into arrogant self-assertion.

But then a reaction follows. As our intercourse with neighbouring peoples is increased we

are struck by their grace, or their versatility, IV.
or their vigour. At once all that is strange in them grows attractive. We endeavour to copy what is not natural to us, that we may gain what we have learnt to admire. We disguise and disparage our own tastes. We assume habits which have not grown out of our circumstances. We treat the characteristic results of our past training as insular prejudices.

It soon however becomes clear that we cannot make others like ourselves or make ourselves like others, and so in our disappointment we aspire to be 'citizens of the world,' regarding with a lofty indifference the various types of human life by which we are surrounded, using and discarding according to our convenience the fashion of the hour, accepting without conviction and abandoning without regret the customs of our neighbourhood, finding nothing more precious or stable in the form of society than in the many tints of earth-born clouds which veil the immeasurable sky.

But here also we are disappointed. This temper brings no satisfaction or rest: we find ourselves dwarfed and chilled by the narrowing of our sympathies. We are poorer, and we feel ourselves to be poorer, as men in proportion as we have succeeded in our endeavours after domi-

IV. nation, imitation, indifference. Happy are we if we confess that these self-willed interpretations of the facts of the world are vain; for then
Eph. i. 18. God opens *the eyes of our hearts* to see a little more of His wider counsel: to see how the principles which bring harmony to the life of the Nation, bring harmony also to the life of the Race: to see how the ideas of fellowship, authority, service, which hallow the relations of the Family and of the state, hallow the relations of the many peoples among whom the manifold endowments of humanity are distributed for the common blessing: to see how He who *made the world and all things therein made of one every nation of men for to dwell on all the face of the earth, having determined their appointed seasons and the bounds of their dwelling, that they should seek God if haply they might feel after Him and find Him:* to see, in other words, that there is a purpose in the rise and fall of empires, in the spread and repression of races, in the varieties of character which are shaped by the conditions of existence: to see that every natural circumstance is designed to lead men to discern God as He is variously present to them and to bring together the fruits of their experience for the further revelation of His
John i. 14. will: to see that when *the Word became flesh* the unity of the race was sealed in a divine fact of life.

So taught we look back, and, guided by the IV.
prophetic records of the Old Testament, we are able to trace how *in many parts and in many fashions* Heb. i. 1.
the riches and the wants of man's nature were laid open before Christ came through Egypt, Persia, Greece, Rome: to trace how since He came the ministry of the nations has in unexpected ways illuminated the truth of the Incarnation.

We look forward, and, through the troubled confusion of arrogance and ambition and selfishness, which distorts the superficial view of politics, we discern that a movement towards a fuller recognition of the kinsmanship of the Race, towards the kingdom of God, is still advancing: that might is learning the authority of righteousness: that privilege is learning the obligation of duty: that the growth of wide dominion is deepening the sense of local responsibility: that the powers of a larger life are beginning to control the passionate outbursts of national feeling.

Such experiences, such thoughts, cannot but affect us as Englishmen most deeply. A conviction not only of the brotherhood of men but of the several offices of the many nations as organs in one body is essential for the hallowing of our national work. If the thought of the common life of humanity is a theory for others, for us it must be the inspiration of duty, of duty which seems to be overwhelming when we realise it. For indeed we may well tremble when we reflect on the common interests of mankind which are perilled in the keeping of England. She stands as no other country stands in a threefold relation to great families of men. She stands face to face with the most powerful empires, as their peer, bound to guard her heritage and to commend to others, by courage, by generosity, by self-control, the blessings which she has received. She stands face to face with the weakest tribes, as their sovereign, bound to protect, to foster, to develop human forces which have not yet reached their full growth. She stands yet again face to face with daughter-peoples, jealous of their independence and loyal in their affection, through whom, as their parent, she is called to mould a new world to sober freedom, not by rigid control but by spiritual quickening. Never has any nation received a charge of authority so far reaching, and so complex. There is not a social problem of the future of which the elements are not included within its range. And if we have to deplore past faults in our dealings with the strong, and the feeble, and the immature, the lessons of past faults have been at least partly mastered. The national conscience has in some degree realised the weight of the nation's burden. Once

and again in late years the bitterness of failure IV.
has been accepted when an easy victory might have satisfied the first cry for revenge. We have learnt at least not to measure our loyalty to justice by the fear of consequences, or our capacity for sacrifice by the hope of material gain.

In this way we have caught, I trust, a faint glimpse of the life of the Race and of the solemn grandeur of the office to which we have been called, far too great for idle pride, and too perilous for complacent self-assertion. Some aspects of it even now are being forced upon our sight with startling effect. Few of us, for example, can have looked on the marvellous products of Indian industries at Kensington, and on the vivid portraiture of the native races there, without feeling that it is a revelation full of sad questionings. One detail, at least, touched me with singular pathos. You will search in vain, I think, in all that multitudinous display of ornament, rich in exquisite harmonies of colour and in delicacy of patient skill, for one trace of reverence for man. Every human form which finds a place there in metal or wood or pottery is either grotesque or hideous, a mockery or a symbol of brute force. And what shall we say?

> Have we not reason to lament
> What man has made of man?

IV. But we have caught, I repeat, a faint glimpse of the office towards mankind to which England has been called: and do we ask, then, what we can do to fulfil it, we here, in our busy, anxious lives? For the present, I answer, it is enough that we should acknowledge the office, that we should dwell upon it, that we should devoutly confess it in the sight of God, that we should make our faith in it the touchstone of our judgments on international policy, that we should strive to extend to our dealings with subject peo-
Is. i. 17. ples the command to *judge the fatherless and plead for the widow;* that we should be careful not to make our power the counsellor of our designs, or our material interests the standard of our successes: that we should brand with the contempt which we feel the cynical assumption that the masses of men respond only to the pressure of fear or the allurements of pleasure: that we should welcome the truth that we hold every endowment which we have received from nature or from discipline in trust for our race, as members of one divine Family, citizens in one Kingdom of God.

The way of action will be made clear as soon as the spirit of action has gained power. When a great idea has grown familiar it is not far from accomplishment. A single nation, moved by one

thought, could alter the fortunes of the world. IV.
And, as has been said by one not of us, 'the power of love as the basis of a state has not yet been tried.' But, if there are prophecies which fulfil themselves, there is also a faith which fulfils itself. The most apostolic man whom I ever saw dared when young to plead the forlorn cause of the American Indians before the Convention of his Church. Every voice was against him: he was confusing, it was urged, politics with religion. Defeated and disheartened, as he told me, he bowed his head upon his hands to hide his tears. Then at length he felt the touch of his senior bishop and heard his words: 'You are right, and you will prevail.' And he has prevailed. The Bishop of Minnesota is now the trusted adviser of the statesmen of the Union.

Yes: the work of God will prevail. The universal claims of man upon man, the cause of humanity will prevail, not perhaps through those to whom it is first committed, and certainly not without suffering. But the issue of the cause is not for us. The cause itself is. It is our inheritance. And as we ponder its splendid promise we shall drive out the spirit of domination by the enthusiasm of service: the spirit of imitation by reverent sympathy: the spirit of indifference by adoring gratitude for the variety of the

IV. divine gifts. We shall grow conscious of the limits of our own powers, and so we shall better understand that God is preparing His kingdom, not through one nation only but through many nations, and claiming from others ministries which we cannot render.

We shall watch with something worthier than idle curiosity or complacent prophesying the convulsions of noble races troubled by evil traditions or yielding under terrible disasters to evil dreams. We shall see that the kingdom of God is hindered, and our own resources impoverished, when the work of any one nation is marred or left undone. We shall know that the true patriot seeks the highest good of his own country, not at the cost of other countries, but through their corresponding advance.

We shall still fear when we think of the burden of empire which has been laid upon us not for material aggrandisement, not for the accumulation of private wealth, not for the suppression of independent growth, but that we may educate to generous activity great peoples in the East and West for the fulfilment of one life. We shall still fear, but in our fear we shall turn to God, *of*
Rom. xi. 36. *whom and through whom and unto whom are all things.*

Words in our Prayer-Book which have seemed

almost meaningless will grow eloquent with each IV.
message that is flashed from scenes of barbarous war or social corruption. We shall pray, as we have never prayed before, that God 'will arise and help us according to the noble deeds which we have heard from our fathers.' We shall pray, with an intense feeling of our own need, 'for all sorts and conditions of men,' 'for all Christian kings, princes, and governors.' We shall pray with a quickened sympathy for the gift of 'peace, unity and concord to all nations.' Every tale of suffering, every threat of vengeance, every record of justice violated and duty abandoned, will breathe power into the petition we bring as children, brethren, to our common Father: *Thy kingdom come.*

Nor can we doubt that the prayer which springs from faith and which is imaged in life will receive an answer. The God of revelation—the Father of our Lord Jesus Christ, the Father of humanity in Christ—is *the God of hope.* And if Rom. xv. 13.
politics too often sadden and distress us, it is because we do not approach questions of statesmanship with a sense of what men are, of what nations are, of what humanity is, in virtue of the Gospel of the grace of God.

All will be changed if we remember that the great counsel, on which we have dwelt, whereby

IV. the Creator *made of one every nation of men for to dwell on all the face of the earth, having determined their appointed seasons and the bounds of their dwelling, that they should seek God,* has found accomplishment in the Son of man, Born, Crucified, Ascended; and that it is for us, for each one of us in our measure, to claim, to use, to spread the blessing of His universal victory, in the strength of His Spirit. The bonds of commerce may prove too weak to hold the peoples together, for they depend upon the variable forces of material interests. The bonds of literature may prove too weak, for they still draw their strength from a part, if it be a nobler part, of man's nature. But the unity of the life in Christ cannot fail our hopes. It has to be recognised and not to be created.

V

THE CHURCH.

...The Church, which is His Body.

EPH. i. 22 f.

THE CHURCH.

WE have seen how man born in a Family is so constituted as to feel after and to find the larger fellowships of the Nation and of the Race, and to bring to these the master principles of life which he has learnt in the sacred circle of home. But there remains yet another fellowship which underlies and sustains all these. Man is born not only for the Family, for the Nation, for the Race, but also for God. He lives in communion with the unseen as well as with the seen. The eternal, to which every outward form of social order ministers in due measure, has its own organ on earth though it is not of earth. That organ is the Church. v.

And when I speak of the Church now I do not propose to enter on any topic of ecclesiastical controversy. I do not propose to touch on the organisation of the Church, its ministry, its services, its sacraments. I wish simply to suggest a few thoughts as to its moral office, as to its universal mission, and as to its embodiment among our-

v. selves. I wish to regard some features of the Church as being, if I may use the phrase, the social revelation of the Holy Spirit, sent to us in Christ's Name, and then some features of our national Church as the organ of our common spiritual life.

The Church is indeed finally the realisation of the brotherhood of men, and it is the abiding pledge of that truth in the face of present separations and rivalries of nations. There has been, we must remember, a Church on the earth, essentially the same in idea and in destination, from the time when Abram the father of the faithful followed the voice of God, as *seeing the invisible,* and rested in the assurance that the blessing of his work was for *all the families of the earth.* (Gen. xii. 1 ff.) When the Divine promise was afterwards held in suspense by the intervention of the Law, even then Israel was charged with an office for all men, *the Church in the wilderness,* (Acts vii. 38.) the Church in Canaan. And throughout the Old Testament we can trace the clear and instructive distinction between 'the people' and 'the nations,' 'the Church' and 'the world,' as we should speak, the one Divine society which God was shaping for Himself, and the many human societies, the outgrowth of the natural development of man, as it was unfolded in the

progress of time under the manifold conditions v.
of human existence. But though the people and the nations were continually brought into the keenest antagonism, they both had offices to fulfil in the education of mankind. And Christ when He came here as elsewhere reconciled what was before in conflict, interpreted what was before obscure, united what was before separate. He was, as we proclaim day by day, *a light for* Luke ii. 32.
revelation to the nations, as well as *the glory of Israel*, the people of the Lord. So Simeon welcomed the Infant Saviour, and, as we have already noticed, the Seer of the Apocalypse saw the fulfilment of that which was thus recognised in its beginning when he beheld the *kings of the* Apoc. xxi. 24.
earth bringing their glory into the city of God.

That is the end: in that vision the Church and the nations are at last one in the open presence of God. But meanwhile, till the end is reached, and that the end may be reached, the Church and the nations have separate works to do in which we all have to take part. To both the Family furnishes the laws of order and the Individual the principle of progress. Both are natural and not artificial combinations of men. Both contribute to the right disciplining of our characters. Both furnish us with opportunities and instruments of fruitful action. We

v. must—to apply the truth to ourselves—strive to remember that we are Christians the more zealously because we remember that we are Englishmen. We must gratefully yield ourselves to the religious influences which are peculiar to our historical position, while we reverently cherish the universal life of our common Faith.

1. What then we ask is the social mission of the Church? The Church has been to the world in every age from the call of Abraham the herald and the witness of the revelation of a living God, of the present reality and power of the unseen and the eternal, of the intercourse of earth and heaven, of the love of the Creator for the world which He created, of the provision which He makes to bring His love to man, of the faith by which man takes that love to himself; and for Christians the Church is the herald and witness and minister of the Incarnation, of the fulfilment of the destiny of man by the Son of God, in which Gospel is the seal of every divine promise, the supply of every human want, the satisfaction of every human hope. And more than this the Church is also the organ of the continuous unfolding of the treasures of spiritual wisdom, as the thoughts of men are purified and widened in the experience of life. And yet again: it is the unwearied preacher of the example, and dispenser of the gifts of Christ.

In the discharge of each of these three offices v.
for sense-bound, wandering, struggling men the Church has one watchword, which marks its strength and its aim, *Sursum corda:* 'Lift up your hearts.'

(*a*) We all know how overwhelming is the power of things outward and visible upon us: how we are engrossed by material cares: stirred by material hopes: diverted if not satisfied by material pleasures: how our world tends to be shut in ever closer and closer by limits of time and place; and how it becomes more exacting as it grows narrower; how earthly excitements, pleasures, even helps to devotion require to be increased in intensity in order that they may produce their effect till they become a crushing load. Then the Church opens to us a larger and serener realm. It holds before us the end for which we were made, even to become like God. It quickens again the noblest thoughts of our hearts by the calm of holydays, by the fellowship of solemn services, by the silent eloquence of stately temples in which the dead still living proclaim the victories of faith: it hallows through the institution of the sacraments every object of sense with something of a sacramental value as a sign of unimaginable glory. It peoples the solitude of our hearts with innumerable hosts

v. of heavenly beings. It makes the communion of saints the pledge of a life of which sight is no measure and no test. It gives us when we look upon the vastness of the sea and the sky and the mountains, instead of a vague feeling of mysterious grandeur, a vision of the Presence of God. It brings home to us the power of
Matt.xviii. 20. Christ's words that He is *with two or three gathered together in His Name.* It does not turn us away from the duties of the world but transfigures them by a new sanctity. It adds an element of infinity to common things. It says to the weary, to the defeated, to the disconsolate, in the prospect of overwhelming evil, 'The end is not yet.'

The Church is the prophet of the eternal in the light of creation.

(*b*) In virtue of this office the Church becomes the òrgan of a continuous apprehension of the will of God. We cannot analyse its action but we can recognise the truths which it brings to light out of the treasury of God. In this way it determined the outlines of our Baptismal Creed: in this way it fixed the contents of our Bible. For these results were gained not by any formal decree of theologians or scholars, not by any deliberate design, but through the force of that common consciousness of the Society which is the voice of the Spirit through the Body of Christ. So the Church has worked in the past: so it is working still. For we can feel how the same divine energy is active about us now, guiding our minds to wiser judgments, guarding us from the dangers of peremptory confidence, keeping open avenues of light which our impatience is ready to close in the presence of new problems, vast in their range and in their promise. For we cannot hide from ourselves that we are called upon to consider new aspects of Nature and Life. And if many seem to tell us that Nature is only what can be measured, counted, weighed, the soul of the Christian Society touched by the Holy Ghost keeps the fulness of truth for our joy. Nature is not exhausted by science: it is not exhausted by art: here also the Spirit has its work to do. And the Church takes Milton's memorable question v.

> What if earth
> Be but the shadow of heaven?

and enables us to feel that by that splendid suggestion we can pass through the seen to the unseen, and give reality to the immeasurable depths of life, and lay the foundations of a social brotherhood on the fuller acknowledgment of the Divine about us. This, I repeat, is a work of the Church now; and no one, I believe, can watch the deep current of contemporary religious opinion, below the storms which trouble its surface,

v. without feeling that God is speaking to us, and that the consciousness of Christendom, in spite of our divisions, is gradually appropriating His message.

The Church is the interpreter of the world in the light of the Incarnation.

(*c*) Then again the Church is above all, as I said, the unwearied preacher of the example of Christ, the appointed organ of the gifts of Christ. It keeps before us through every failure the undying record of the victory of love. It shews us the accomplishment of man's destiny through suffering. Arrogance may lift its front among us; indolent idleness may squander its treasure: the strong may assert their self-sufficiency, and the privileged may deny their obligations: but the arrogant, the indolent—the confidence of strength and the isolation of privilege—are alike condemned, so that all men can see their sentence, in the vision of Him who reigns from the Cross. In the presence of that Vision, which every Christian society offers for the adoration of its children, reverence, labour, dependence, service are recognised by the soul as the marks of the social life which is established in Christ, and which draws from Him its motion, its benediction, and its support.

For while the Christian society offers us an

ideal, it supplies us with the power to strive towards it. It exercises a spiritual influence which works surely and silently. It preserves a perennial connexion with the source of Divine strength. It offers us the gift of life, the gift of the Holy Spirit, the gift of the virtue of Christ's Humanity, according to His own appointment. It guards us from the perils of subjective fanaticism by the calm strength of an outward organisation. v.

When the understanding fails and every appearance tends to sadden us, it keeps the great assurance fresh: *I, if I be lifted up*—victorious John xii. 32.
over death, victorious through death—*will draw*—by the omnipotence of an endless compassion which subdues the rebellious soul—*all men unto me.*

The Church is the quickener and sustainer of life in the light of the Redemption.

2. Such is the universal mission of the Church, and in every nation the mission must be fulfilled according to the peculiar circumstances of the national history and of the national character. And if the nation is, as we hold, a living whole, its constitution will be incomplete if it has no organ for the development and for the expression of its spiritual powers: if it has not, in other words, a national Church.

No one can acknowledge more heartily than

V. I do the services which isolated Christian societies in England have rendered to personal religion. They have insisted with victorious resolution on the sacredness of individual conviction. They have maintained a high standard of individual effort. But this individual aspect of the Faith is not all. Christianity is a social power as well as an individual power. It is presented to us from the very first as embodied in a kingdom. A national Church alone can consecrate the whole life of the people. A national Church alone can bring to every citizen the ministrations of religion, not as offering a voluntary gift but as satisfying a rightful claim.

Now no one will question that the Church of England occupies a historical position which is without parallel. It has borne with the nation the pressure of foreign conquest and domestic revolution, and drawn breadth and vigour from both. It has received the treasures of alien thought and experience, and vindicated its independence. It has never broken with the past and yet it has put off the accretions of age. But I concede at once that we cannot support its claims by its history if its fruits do not answer to its growth. If our national Church does not proclaim a faith which is the soul of our corporate life: if it does not use for the common good an inheritance which is unique and inestimable: if it does not accept a responsibility which no other society admits: then I allow that no prescription, no gratitude, no past victories, can justify our allegiance to that which has now lost its virtue. v.

Here again however it is clear that the Church of England does externally at least stand out as a witness to our common Faith. It embodies a principle and a power: the principle that religion is an element in the highest national life, the power of a catholic sympathy. It proclaims before the world that our government acknowledges a Divine sovereignty. It undertakes the task of coming to all with the message of the Gospel.

And if it be said that it has failed in its mission: that its representatives have not spoken out boldly in Christ's Name on this occasion and that: that the Truth has not been brought by it effectively to the dense population of our towns; I confess that many such accusations are true. I confess that the Church of England has failed, if it be failure to fall short of the ideal. The Church of England has failed as Christianity itself has failed. It has failed through the imperfection of the men who have represented it. But it has not failed so as to

v. abdicate its charge. It has not failed so as to suppress or to dissemble the message which is the condemnation of its shortcomings, or to withhold the gifts which it is commissioned to minister. It has not failed so as to leave its destination without witness. It has not failed so as to refuse to recognise every new claim which has been made upon its service.

And therefore at the present time the national Church stands before us rich with unused resources of power which God has provided for the necessities of this later age; and we who believe unfeignedly in its future, who believe in its mission and in its grace, rejoice to have learnt in some degree the secret of its past failures. And if I am asked to say what this is in the briefest possible form, I reply without hesitation that it is chiefly that we have forgotten the thought which is expressed in the words which I have taken for my text. We have forgotten that the Church is a Body in which an appropriate office belongs to every member; and so we have suffered grievously from a loss of power and from a loss of mutual understanding.

We have suffered grievously from loss of power. Those who are set to be teachers among us, who need ample leisure for calm reading and high thinking in order that they may follow the swift currents of opinion, have been overwhelmed with labours not their own, with anxieties of finance and with details of parish organisation. v. And those again who have a practical knowledge of affairs, a wide influence in business, a rich endowment of 'saving common sense' have found no proper sphere for the exercise of their gifts. The clergy by the force of circumstances have added the work of the laity to their own; and the laity left without work have, almost of necessity, remained without zeal.

We have suffered grievously also from a loss of mutual understanding, from the want of a free interchange of opinion between all the classes of which the Church is composed. We of the clergy are apt to regard things from a theoretical point of view without a due sense of proportion. You, brethren, of the laity try thought by a rough standard of practice without a clear discernment of the value of opinion.

We ask then for the free and healthy service of every one that our Church may have her perfect work. The hand cannot delegate its office to the eye or the eye to the heart. If the Church is to fulfil its social functions there must not be a single person in it without a ministry for others. And again if we strive on both

v. sides to enter a little more into the feelings of one another, clergy and laity, to acknowledge frankly our common aims and our common duties, to claim help and to concede authority, there will be a double gain. We on our part shall learn more and more to direct our teaching to *the weightier matters of the law, judgment and mercy and faith*, and you in turn will learn to give a juster value to that exactness of doctrine which is found to be efficacious in conduct.

Matt. xxiii. 23.

This is not the time to suggest the forms which effort should take. Perhaps, if the opportunity be given me, I may do this on some other occasion. Now it must be enough to say, that there are works for 'fathers' answering to the ripeness of wisdom. There are works for 'young men' answering to the enthusiasm of strength. There are works for women answering to the power of sympathy. Let each one here interpret the voice which comes to the individual heart and follow it to fulfilment. A little sacrifice creates a new interest in that which has been undertaken. Having done something we shall find it easier to do more. Unexpected ways will be opened to us by which we shall be enabled to bring our experience and endowments to the service of our Church, to the service of Christ.

And such service will react upon our own spiritual life. Life becomes nobler and happier as the sympathies and offices of life are enlarged. It is at first an awful thing to know that the voice which we hear is indeed the voice of God. But he has the strength of a prophet who meets it in due time with the offer of himself. V.

Again then I ask for the willing service of every one. Through us as a Society, through us as organs, each of some special work, Christ is offered to the nation, to the nation with its subject provinces and its daughter states; and the *increase of the Body* comes *through that which* Eph.iv.16.
every joint supplieth.

There are, no doubt, arrears to be made up; but already there are signs of quickened and manifold activity which give abundant promise for the future. And more is at stake in the effects of our combined labour than we are inclined to suppose. The conquest of doubt will come through the conquest of life. Let it be seen that what we have received and what we hold enables us to enter with kindlier interest into the struggles of our neighbours; to join one with another in heartier fellowship for the pursuit of noble ends; to discern with readier intelligence the way of lasting progress; to crush down our besetting selfishness and yet to preserve the

v. individual differences with which we have been endowed; to strive without impatience and without weariness that those with whom we have to do may be a little better for our influence; to make it evident that we do believe in an actual communion between earth and heaven; to live, in a word, by faith; and the issue cannot be uncertain or far distant. What we hold as Christians, what we hold as Churchmen, has, I believe, this power; and it is the part of every one among us to help others to recognise the greatness of the treasure which has been committed to our keeping not for ourselves but for the whole Nation, and not for the Nation only but for the whole Body of Christ.

II.

CHRISTIAN ASPECTS OF THE ORGANISATION OF SOCIAL LIFE.

I. *The Kingdom of God.*

II. *Mediæval efforts: the Franciscans (Francis of Assisi).*

III. *Modern efforts: the Quakers (George Fox).*

IV. *Present Problems.*

The kingdom of God is not eating and drinking, but righteousness and peace and joy in the Holy Ghost.

ROM. xiv. 17.

I. *THE KINGDOM OF GOD.*

'THE Kingdom of heaven,' 'the Kingdom of I.
God,' 'the Kingdom of Christ'—few phrases
are more familiar to us than these: few phrases,
if we pause to reflect upon them, are more intelli-
gible, more eloquent, more impressive. They
bring vividly before us the primitive conception
of the embodiment of the Gospel. They express
what is offered in Scripture from the first page
of Genesis to the last page of the Apocalypse, as
the end of the Divine education of the world.
They epitomize the record of the Lord's life, and
of the work of His apostles. As a King Christ
received His earliest homage in the manger at Matt. ii. 11.
Bethlehem. As a King He died, 'reigning from
the Cross.' The message which His herald was Matt. iii. 2.
commissioned to proclaim, the message with which Matt. iv. 17.
He Himself opened His Ministry, was the Advent
of the Kingdom. After His resurrection He
spoke with His disciples *the things pertaining to* Acts i. 3.
the Kingdom of God. And they in turn carried
the glad-tidings wherever they went beyond the

I. borders of Judæa. It was of a Kingdom St Philip
Acts viii. 12; xiv. spoke at Samaria: of a Kingdom St Paul spoke at
22; xvii. Antioch, Thessalonica, Ephesus. And the last
7; xix. 8; xx. 25. historic glimpse which we have of the apostolic
working shews us the same 'prisoner of the Lord'
Acts preaching the Kingdom of God in his captivity at
xxviii. 23, 31. Rome. In every part of the New Testament, in every region of early Christian labour, the teaching is the same. The object of Redemption is set before us not simply as the deliverance of individual souls but as the establishment of a Divine Society: the saving not only of men but of the world, the hallowing of life and not characteristically the preparation for leaving it.

This thought of the Kingdom was, indeed, the moral of the Old Testament, the issue to which all the training of God's chosen people tended. From the first call of their father Abraham to their last struggle with foreign invaders the same lesson was being enforced upon them in many ways. By bondage and wandering, by conquest and oppression, by brilliant triumphs, by heroic sufferings, by desolate exile, by painful return, the Jews were taught to lift their thoughts to the contemplation of a Divine Sovereignty. They were brought into contact with the great nations of the East, and so they learnt to feel the essen-

tial weakness of the powers beneath which they I.
had fallen for a time only to rise again still stronger. They themselves received a dynasty, in answer to their prayers, which in its first glory seemed to realise by the ways of earth all for which they hoped. But the kingdom of David rapidly descended to the level of human monarchies, and served only to furnish the imagery in which the aspirations of later prophets were clothed. So the hope which had been brought home to the mind of the people, became, in its promise and in its failure, fruitful in greater hopes. Step by step the full majesty of the Divine ideal was realised in thought, while the organisation of material forces was pressed forward with relentless vigour by Roman conquest. At last, in the fulness of time, the contrast between 'the Kingdom of Heaven,' founded on the eternal basis of truth and justice, and the kingdom of the world, which was the final expression of force and self-will, stood revealed. The one was recognised in the sovereignty of love welcomed by faith, and seen in the Person of *the Word become flesh:* the other stood out in the isolation of victorious might, with a deified man as the supreme object of human devotion.

Thus the Gospel of Christ was in its announcement and in its preparation, as it is in its

I. essence, *the Gospel of the Kingdom.* To *seek the*
Matt. iv. 23. *Kingdom* [*of God*] *and His righteousness* is en-
Matt. vi. 33. joined upon the believer as his first duty; and we ourselves at least in word acknowledge the obligation. Morning and Evening we all pray in Christ's own words that 'Our Father's Kingdom may come, on earth as in heaven': that it may 'come,' not that we may be carried away to it far off, out of this stormy tumult of common cares as to some tranquil haven of rest: that it may come to us 'on earth as in heaven.' For the Kingdom of God is at once spiritual and historical: eternal and temporal: outward and inward: visible and invisible: a system and an energy. It is an order of things in which heavenly laws are recognised and obeyed. It depends both for its origin and for its support upon forces which are not of earth. It is inspired by the principles and powers of a higher sphere. It implies a harmonious relation between men and the beings of the unseen universe (*the Kingdom of Heaven*). It places its members in a social and personal relationship to a Divine Head, as citizens to a King, as children to a Father ('*the Kingdom of God*,' '*the Kingdom of your Father which is in heaven*').

But at the same time, though it is not limited by the conditions of our present existence, it is manifested under them. It is in the world though

it is not of the world. The scene on which it is I.
shewn to be realised is the scene of human life. The Lord speaks habitually of His coming again, of His Presence, and in one sense He fixes the Matt. xvi. 28.
time of His Coming in the generation of those whom He addressed. He points forward, if I may gather up what I would say in one sentence, to a transfiguration of human society which corresponds to the Resurrection of the individual.

Yes, this is Christ's teaching; and we believe the fulness of His promise: we acknowledge the universality of His work. He did not come to found a school by unfolding new forms of intellectual truth: He did not come to mould a sect by the imposition of an outward rule. He came to deal with the whole of life, with thought, action, feeling, with life in its largest and noblest forms, with life in every phase of its progressive activity. He came to bring a message to the strong and the wealthy and the gay, as well as to the weary and the heavy-laden. He came to found a Kingdom into which *the kings of the earth should* Apoc. xxi. 24.
bring their glory. And for us that Kingdom, the Kingdom of heaven, the Kingdom of God, the Kingdom of the Son of man, is a present reality. We live in it, and yet we look for it. We live in it as recognising the supremacy of a Divine law, the rule of a Divine sovereign, the constitution of a Divine

I. Church. We look for it, as we wait for *the re-*
Rom. viii. 23. *demption of our own bodies.* Meanwhile we are bound by the obligations of its citizenship, heirs of its glories, sharers in its destiny.

What then are the signs by which our loyalty as citizens of the kingdom of God will be proved? Not any uniform, which can be laid aside when we enter our secret chamber: not any watch-word, which we can learn by an easy tradition; but a character which clothes itself in deeds, a creed which is translated into a life. The citizen must according to the measure of his powers embody the notes of the kingdom. And the *Kingdom of God is not eating and drinking, but righteousness and peace and joy in the Holy Ghost.* It is the social incorporation of a spirit, which penetrates and hallows every region of human activity, of a spirit which consecrates for the common service every variety of heritage and endowment, which combines in a harmonious union the manifold energies of enterprise, which crowns every faithful servant with a blessedness which none can take away or disturb.

'*Righteousness, peace, joy*': the human heart welcomes these three characteristics as marking the society which answers the promise of creation. In these three, that memorable triad, the battle-cry of revolution, which, in spite of every per-

version and misuse, has found a wide response in I.
the souls of nations, receives its highest fulfilment. In 'righteousness, peace, joy' we can recognise 'equality, liberty, fraternity,' interpreted, purified, extended. They tell us that the community and not the individual is the central thought in the life of men. They tell us that the fulfilment of duties and not the assertion of rights is the foundation of the social structure. They tell us that the end of labour is not material well-being, but that larger, deeper, more abiding delight which comes from successfully ministering to the good of others. They tell us that over all that is transitory in the form of the kingdom, over all the conditions which determine its growth, there rest the light, the power, of an Eternal Presence.

'*Righteousness, peace, joy*': these are, I repeat, the Christian translation of Equality, Liberty, Fraternity, in which nothing of the old truth is lost, and all is transfigured. Equality may be so presented as to destroy the richness and the beauty of life. An equality of units in an aggregate carries with it sterile monotony. Life endures no such equality which obliterates the past. But when we say '*Our Father*' there is opened a vision of that true equality which takes form as righteousness in every relation of life. The varie-

I. ties of gifts and circumstances among men are the conditions of mutual service. Our highest is not our own: how then that which is less? But all that we have received and all that we have gained is a trust to be used in the Master's cause. And His will is *that all men should be saved, and come to the knowledge of the truth.* Here therefore is the measure of our duty, the destination of our possessions. Each fellow-man is by God's will made for eternal life, made to discipline and cultivate his powers, made to serve his race and learn the end of his service; and we are bound, as far as lies in us, to strive that each shall attain his end. His cause is our own. Every inequality of earth is lost in the equality of souls. And the temple of the soul—the shrine and the precinct—claims even in its ruins the tender reverence of restoring love.

1 Tim. i. 4.

Liberty again may rapidly degenerate into license. It becomes by an easy transition a specious name for individual caprice and self-assertion. Then the calm strength of the whole is lost in innumerable fragments. But when we say '*Our Father*,' there is opened a vision of that true liberty, the obedience of His perfect law, which is the spring of peace. Caprice is excluded by a living sense of responsibility. Self-assertion is overcome by loyal devotion to a higher rule.

Authority and freedom are reconciled by the thought of a living God. For the barrenness of egoism: for the weakness of self-indulgence: comes the invigorating, controlling faith in the Divine purpose which enjoins upon all the freest development of personal powers, and inspires the independent toiler with that completeness of self-surrender wherein alone there is rest. I.

Yet again fraternity may be made the pretext for imposing upon the weaker, the younger, the less mature, in the family of men, practices and opinions for which they are not prepared, or even for arresting the growth of the more advanced. But when we say '*Our Father,*' there is opened a vision of that true fraternity, the fact of a common spiritual parentage, which brings to all the children the earnest of eternal joy. 'Man,' it has been nobly said, 'is the pleasure of man.' 'A living man,' in the words of an early father, 'is the glory of God.' In every brother, that is, partner in our life, our hope, our end, we have a revelation of the Father's love, offered for our study, for our care, for our thanksgiving. No jealousy can find a place in the fellowship of brethren. No rivalry can trouble the labour of sons who owe everything and bring everything to Him *in Whose Presence is the fulness of joy.* (Iren. *adv. hær.* iv. 20, 7.)

'*Righteousness, peace, joy*': these, I say, are

I. the notes of the Divine Kingdom. But you will ask, Where are they to be found? What society can shew them written on its history or embodied in its life? For the enthusiasm of righteousness and the spontaneous devotion of service and the measuring our work by our capacity, there is on every side submission to an outward ordinance, the discharge of the letter of our bond, the satisfaction of our wants: for the stability of peace and the free concurrence of multitudinous forces and the sure balance of trustful hearts, there is the armed truce where fear witnesses to injustice, the murmuring helplessness of exhaustion, the torpor of tolerant indifference: for the still depths of joy and the vision of a growing dawn and the light of a heavenly Presence, there is the turbulent restlessness of excitement, and the deadening materialism of indulgence.

I know the terrible indictment. I do not disguise or extenuate one dark trait in it. How can I when every morning brings a fresh arraignment of men and nations? But what then? Can it be shewn that the Gospel of the Kingdom has failed in one least point to vindicate its claims? Do we abandon any thing of the splendour of our hope? Christians indeed have been unrighteous, tyrannical, morose; but their Faith is their accuser and their judge. We have

fallen short of our ideal, but we none the less I.
cling to it with inextinguishable desire. And our Faith justifies our confidence. For Faith in the Kingdom of God has entered into life. It has established itself among us in principle and in beginning. It is our Faith in fact which stirs us with passionate discontent: which disciplines us: which assures us that even through our falls we are brought nearer to our goal if only our faces are set towards the light.

'*Righteousness, peace, joy*': where are they to be found? I reply that on us, on all of us, is laid the duty of shewing that these are indeed the notes of the Kingdom to which we belong: the Kingdom which satisfies the social instincts of men. For men are waiting for our work. The social embodiment of the Faith answers to the peculiar temper of the age. Each age has its own difficulties and trials, its own sorrows and doubts, its own aspirations and intuitions of truth. Nor can we doubt in which direction the current of present thought is setting. Never before has there been so wide and keen a sense of the unity of life, of social dependence, of the obligation to determine our mutual relations by duties rather than by rights. Never has the call to labour, to love, to sacrifice, to association, to the acceptance of a common belief and a

I. common aim been so loud or so general. Never has the failure of material remedies for distress made the want of a spiritual force, active and visible among men, so obviously urgent. But such feelings, desires, confessions, are vague and scattered and even discordant. Still they are sincere; and I believe that the 'Gospel of the Kingdom of God,' in its breadth and its simplicity, is able, is alone able, to interpret and to answer and to support every hope and every effort of men, who even from a far country are turning to their common Father.

I believe it: every Christian must believe it. But we cannot be surprised if those who stand without, either in sad or in bitter alienation from us, say, 'Shew us your works.' 'Shew us your works': Brethren, I pray that we may not decline the challenge in whatever spirit it is offered. I pray that we may, God helping us, shew, so that men may see, what the Gospel of the Kingdom, the social Gospel, is. But, that we may do so, it will not be enough to shew, as it can easily be shewn, that whatever is noblest and most inspiring in art, whatever is loftiest and tenderest in thought, whatever is most generous and sovereign in action, whatever is purifying in sorrow and lasting in pleasure, is essentially Christian. It will not be enough to shew that

every crime and every failure of Christians is I.
treason against their faith, and that no good throughout the world is alien from it. We must make it clear, clear in a shape which will strike the imagination of the multitude, that the notes of the Christian Society are 'righteousness, peace, joy.'

We must, I say, make it clear that the notes of the Christian society are 'righteousness, peace, joy.' This is the subject which I wish to commend to your meditation and your prayers during this Advent Season. I propose therefore to consider on the next two Sundays how men sought to gain the end in earlier times, with what failures and what encouragements. And then I hope to suggest on the last Sunday of the year some lessons which we may learn from past experience in dealing with the problems of our own day.

If the work to which we look were to be wrought by human power, I should not dare to speak. But it is the work of God. He is pleased to work through us, but He Himself works. The righteousness, the peace, the joy, which we are charged to make our own and to bring to the world are *in the Holy Ghost.* They are the revelation of His Spirit *in Whom we live* Acts xvii.
and move and have our being. We are not called 28.
to found, but to *receive a Kingdom,* a Kingdom Hebr. xii.
that cannot be shaken. Our part is only to offer 28.

I. ourselves to the Divine influence by which we are surrounded: to listen to the still Voice which speaks in our souls with whisperings which if they cannot be uttered yet cannot be misunder-
Hebr. vi. 5. stood: to use the powers of the new age.

Oh, my friends, life is vaster, immeasurably vaster, than we think, richer in resources, more fertile in strength, more blessed in opportunity. The glory of the Lord is still about the pilgrim's path: the Saviour, in His Spirit, is still with
Luke xxiv. 16. us, though *our eyes are holden that we should not know Him.*

We read that of old time, when the servant of the lonely prophet found that his master was encompassed by a vast host of pitiless enemies,
2 Kings vi. 15 ff. he cried, *Alas, my master! how shall we do? And he answered, Fear not: for they that be with us, are more than they that be with them. And Elisha prayed, and said, Lord, I pray thee, open his eyes, that he may see. And the Lord opened the eyes of the young man; and he saw: and, behold, the mountain was full of horses and chariots of fire about Elisha.*

Even so it is now. We too are moving a-
Hebr. xii. 22. midst the legions of light: *we are come unto the city of the living God, the heavenly Jerusalem*; but our sight is dim and our faith is feeble. Lord, we pray Thee, open our eyes that we may see.

II.

MEDIÆVAL EFFORTS: THE FRANCISCANS (FRANCIS OF ASSISI).

Blessed are the poor.

St Luke vi. 20.

Blessed are the poor in spirit.

St Matt. v. 3.

II. *THE FRANCISCANS.*

THERE are periods in the history of the II.
Church—the history of the spiritual growth of humanity—which are at once an end and a beginning. The material forms of civilisation grow old, and the life which they have at once protected and expressed takes a new shape. Unexpected forces reveal themselves. Unexpected evils make themselves felt. Such periods are periods of intense, disordered, passionate feeling, *men's hearts failing them for fear, and for ex-* Luke xxi. 26.
pectation of the things which are coming on the world. They are, in the language of Scripture, periods of a new birth, full of the anguish of John xvi. 21 f.
travail and yet sustained by the assurance of a greater joy. They are periods in which Christ is pleased to come to His people with some new revelation of His sovereign purpose and power.

Such a period was the beginning of the thirteenth century. It was a crisis of dissolution and a revelation of strength. The foundations of the life of modern Europe, social,

II. political, intellectual, religious, were laid there silently and deeply, laid in tribulation and perplexity, laid by men who knew not whereunto their work would grow. The Crusades, which had been undertaken in the hope of crowning a united Christendom with a decisive triumph, had brought very different results. It seemed as if the West would be converted by the East.

The corruption of Oriental life, the influence of Oriental speculation, spread like a flood over the divided and disorganised Christian kingdoms. But meanwhile the power of the commons was being consolidated. Commercial republics became in the North the home of freedom, and in the South the nurseries of Art. Guilds of craftsmen were developed. Colleges of scholars were founded. Vernacular literature began to rise on the ruins of Latin. Above all, nations grew to the consciousness of a common life.

In these movements we can see now the earnest of a better order than the premature unity of the Empire and the Papacy. But there was a terrible dark side to the age. The leprosy which was then the terror and the scourge of the towns was the symbol of evils greater and more subtle which were eating into the heart of society. The Kingdom of God was on the point of becoming a kingdom of the world. The splendid churches which serve for the inspiration of modern art were too often built by extortion. Religion was materialised both in its Creed and in its worship. Ecclesiastical jurisdiction was invading the whole sphere of life. The very consolations of the faith were being degraded into a luxury for the wealthy. The poor—the poor on whom Christ pronounced His first benediction—were in danger of being forgotten. II.

But the Spirit of Christ was not left without witness. Preachers arose on many sides who vindicated for the Kingdom of God the claim to *righteousness and peace and joy.* For the most part their work was transitory because it was destructive, but one among them, Francis of Assisi, spoke in life, so that his work can never cease to move. He built up, purified, ennobled what he found, overcoming evil by the good. Through Francis of Assisi the mediæval efforts after the Kingdom of God found their most characteristic embodiment. Of him then I wish to speak this afternoon, while the echoes of his Hymn of Creation, the most perfect expression of his heart, still linger in our Abbey.

Bright, joyous, enterprising, thoughtlessly lavish by nature, untrained in scholastic learning, instinct with poetic enthusiasm, Francis came to

II. men simply as a man. He knew but one pattern,
Ap. 50. the Lord Himself. He knew but one lesson, the story of the Cross. His call reached him under the forms of the popular activity of the time. He heard in a vision that an inestimable prize was to be won by his warfare. Forthwith he sought military service only to learn that he must be the soldier of Christ. A voice came to him as he lay prostrate in a church falling to decay and bade him restore the ruins which he saw. At once he sacrificed all that he had and laboured with his own hands to repair the material fabric, only to learn that he must build up a spiritual temple. While he was pondering in his heart the nature of his future work he is said to have received a sign which interpreted it. He came suddenly upon a leper. The sight filled him with horror. But he remembered that the first victory of the true conqueror must be over himself. So when the miserable outcast stretched forth his hand for alms Francis added a kiss to his gift and then passed on. Shortly afterwards he looked round; but there was no leper in the wide plain, and he
p. 45. knew that he had seen the Lord. 'When I was 'in sin,' he writes in his testament, dictated on his death-bed, 'it was a sore trial to me to see 'lepers; but the Lord Himself brought me to 'them, and I wrought mercy upon them; and

'when I left them, my trial was turned to de- II.
'light of soul and body.'

That was the secret which Francis had to disclose. He placed himself on the level of the most abject and found *peace and joy* in the completeness of devotion. He offered to the simple, outward faith of the middle ages, in a shape which they could not fail to understand, a visible image of love, of love to God and love to man. He brought Christ out of the student's cell into the wild and sordid conflicts of life. He was, if I may so speak, a living *Imitatio Christi.* Self was lost in the call. He threw himself wholly upon God. 'Multiply my pains a hundredfold, p. 43.
'O Lord,' was his prayer in sickness, 'if it please 'Thee. The fulfilling of Thy holy will is consolation more than enough.' He sought and touched the leper in body or in soul. 'Are you 'thinking of a bride?' said a friend lightly when he stood suddenly silent under the still night. 'Yes,' he replied, 'of a bride nobler, richer, 'more beautiful than your fancy can conceive.' And so he took to him Poverty, or rather Humanity bleeding from a thousand wounds, 'whom none had chosen for his own since 'Christ Himself,' to cherish to his life's end with unfailing tenderness. In that mystic companionship he stood like a prophet of old 'a sign and

II. a wonder' to a proud and turbulent and luxurious age.

The power of the example soon made itself felt. Francis drew to him without effort and without any conscious plan a few followers who found in the new life the Gospel for which they looked, the Gospel for the poor. No wretchedness was too deep for their hope: no effort was too great for their faith. They did not affect the
Reg. ii. § 2. right of judging others: it was enough to bless God for what He had taught them. They sought to teach by deed rather than by word, yet not so as to appear better than their fellow men. Their
Coll. 12. hope was to lift the fallen up to a higher level by quickening the germ of life within them through the spectacle of God's power in themselves.

In this way their work grew with amazing rapidity. The brethren were sent to and fro in every direction with the salutation of peace to bear the message of repentance and faith abroad. They went as missionaries to the Saracens, and, above all, as missionaries to the miserable multitudes who sought shelter in the large towns. They settled among the lowest. Once again they brought thought into life, and theology to the people. The peace of the cloister, securely guarded from the storms of common cares, had no charm for them. They would win peace in the market

and in the crowd. And they won it by self-sacri- II.
fice. 'You ask me', Francis said, 'whether prayer *Coll.* 14.
'or preaching is more pleasing to God. It is a 'hard question...In praying we speak to God and 'hear Him, and live, as it were with angels, the 'life of angels: in preaching we must bring our'selves down to a low level in dealing with men, 'and live among them in the ways of men, and 'think men's thoughts and see with men's eyes, 'and hear and use men's words. But one con'sideration is decisive. The only Son of God 'came down from the Bosom of the Father for 'the salvation of souls. We, too, must follow 'His pattern. We must give up our quiet and 'go forth to toil.'

Such teaching, such lives, stirred the masses of men. Crowds of eager inquirers gathered round Francis and demanded what they must do, bound as they were by the duties of home and state? In answer to their prayers he drew up a rule for
men and women living in the world. Those who pp. 94 ff.
subscribed it were bound to renounce all ill-gotten gains: to abstain from aggressive war, and litigation: to observe the utmost simplicity in dress and intercourse and amusements: to give themselves according to their opportunity to works of devotion: to meet from time to time for common worship and almsgiving. There was nothing

II. strained or fantastic in the provisions which promised consecration and calm and dignity to ordinary life. The rule was widely embraced throughout Christendom by people of every rank. Louis of France and Elizabeth of Hungary were among the first royal persons who were enrolled under it, and a multitude of poor were united with them in one sacred fellowship of service. It was a startling innovation on the current conceptions of holy living. In a solemn and striking form, open to the eyes of all men, the likeness of Christ was recognised as attainable through the offices and powers of every station.

By the institution of this Third Order of 'the brothers and sisters of penitence', as they were called, the work of Francis was consummated. It seemed for a short space as if the Kingdom of God were indeed about to be established on earth. Then followed a swift decline. Even in the lifetime of Francis the simplicity of his rule was marred. After his death came the corruptions of ambition and controversy. Mendicancy was made the rule instead of the exception. Fictions were devised to justify the acceptance of property. The privileges of the secular clergy were disregarded. The Franciscans disputed with the Dominicans the supremacy of the schools, and carried Theology back to words. But even while the Order failed to realise the ideal of their founder, the spiritual forces which he had called out were still fertile for good. The intense sympathy of Francis with the life of Nature gave a fresh impulse to art, and the splendid church which rose over his tomb within seventeen years of his death received some of the earliest treasures of Italian painting, and fresh masters, as they rose to fame, delighted to add their tribute to his honour. Francis had discouraged learning, but his scholars were forced to meet the keen questionings of men for whom life was a real battle. In such encounters they were disciplined in the search for knowledge and in the use of it. Day by day, in the streets and the hospitals, they were forced to consider the changing circumstances of life, and to deal with sickness and suffering. In such service they learnt to question nature patiently, and laid the foundation of inductive science. In thought and work the sense of a divine communion was their strength, and they kindled in innumerable homes that fire of piety which saved Europe in the age of the Renaissance.

II. *Coll.* 15.

But still the Order, as a type of the Divine Kingdom, failed, and I believe that it was doomed to failure by the very principles of its Founder. Francis aimed at an ideal which ne-

II. glected essential facts of life. He sought to destroy individuality. It is said that he once ordered a disobedient brother to be stripped and placed in an open grave. The earth was then heaped round him, and when his head alone was uncovered, Francis came near and said, 'Art thou
Colloqu. 40. dead, brother? art thou dead?' 'Yes,' the penitent replied, 'I am dead now.' 'Rise then,' he said, '... I will have dead men, not living, for my followers.' Francis paused, that is, at the first stage in the transformation of the Christian. The death of perfect self-surrender is the condition of resurrection to the power of a new life; but life, deeper, fuller, intenser, must flow from the completed sacrifice. Every gift, every faculty, every circumstance of personal being is transformed by that death, and given back to be used with nobler energy and keener responsibility. The living God seeks the service of living men.

Francis disregarded the sacred individuality of men. He disregarded also the divine office of nations for the race. He strove, in a word, to seize the conception of humanity without recognising the form of life through which God is pleased to reveal to us the rich fulness of the whole. So it came to pass that his Friars were made from the first the agents of papal exac-

tions, the servants and representatives in each II.
country of a foreign power.

Yet once again the tender devotion of Francis to the Lord's manhood became the occasion of grievous error. Everything that is compassionate in the character of the Lord was separated from His sovereign righteousness, and then these attributes of tender love were transferred to His human Mother, who seemed to be more within the reach of rude and simple minds. In this way a system of Mariolatry was shaped, with what consequence they know who were familiar with the popular religion of modern Italy. Even Francis himself was set by some in the place of the Lord. The evil spread far and wide; and many who hear me must have looked with shuddering, as I have looked, on a picture at Brussels, painted by Rubens for the Franciscan Church at Ghent, in which Francis and the Mother of the Lord are shielding the world from the thunderbolts which the Divine Son is directing against it.

The Order of Francis failed in its issue, and it is well to take account of the causes of its failure; but it is far more welcome to mark the causes of its first splendid success, and to contemplate in that spontaneous homage of multitudes the infinite power of humility, of sympathy, of sacrifice, of faith.

II. *Colloqu.* 12. 'Why is it, father,' said one of his first companions to Francis, 'that all the world goes after you?' 'Why,' he replied, 'even for this: the Lord saw no greater sinner in the world, none less wise, none viler, and so He chose me above all to accomplish a wonderful work in the earth.' *Ap.* 36; comp. 19. 'If God were to take from me the treasures of His Grace which He has lent me, what else should I have but body and soul, common to the faithful and the unbeliever alike?'

Such a spirit of enthusiastic humility cannot but become an inexhaustible source of sympathy. He who feels what God has done for himself, *Colloqu.* 14. has a measure of what He is ready to do. 'My brothers,' Francis said to some of his Order who were discouraged by ill-treatment, 'you will convert all men by your word, if in all things you humble yourselves': if, that is, you enter into the secret of the souls of those whom you approach, if you place yourselves lovingly beside them, if you enable them to feel that all that there is in you of purity and patience and graciousness is theirs as well as yours, because it is God's only and wholly. And at the same time this perfect self-abasement becomes the solid ground *Ex.* 5. of self-reverence. When, on another occasion, some of the companions of Francis were scandalised because he allowed the crowds to kiss his feet, he answered, 'This honour is not to me, but to God.' From such reverence, be sure, men gain great good while they acknowledge God in His creatures. He is not unaware of God in himself who recognises Him in a creature. II.

But not to multiply illustrations, over which the heart loves to linger, three main lessons seem to be pressed upon us by the work of Francis, the capacity of simple humanity for the highest joys of life, so that the poorest even in his utter destitution may realise the bliss of saints; and again the necessity of taking account of the fulness and variety of life in our endeavours to hasten the Kingdom of God: and yet again the importance of the mission of the laity.

We need sorely all three lessons now. We need, from the highest to the lowest, to feel the essential dignity of life, of life stripped of every accidental vesture; the dignity of the living man, clothed in the coarsest cloke of patches and fed on fragments, who can look with open eyes to God and call Him 'Father.' We need, from the highest to the lowest, to feel the perilous burden of wealth, the responsibility of stewardship, the cares of authority. Francis lost nothing of his grace and courtesy, nothing of his joyousness, nothing of his delight in Sun and Moon and Wind and Fire and Earth, because he had cast off

II. every perishable help towards sustaining such gifts in their freshness. When the Bishop of Assisi warned him of the troubles to which he exposed himself in refusing to have any goods: 'Nay, *Ap.* 21. Cf. Bonav. IV. § 6, p. 333. rather,' he said, 'I think the trouble is in having them; for such is the anxiety of defending your possessions that you must be prepared to settle the disputes which they engender by force of arms.'

We need, in other words, to know the blessedness of *the poor, the poor in spirit:* to know that Luke xii. 15. our life cometh not of our possessions in their abundance; but lies deep below the penury which sees the Invisible face to face, deep below the wealth which is given through men to God, our *Col.* iii. 3. life in Christ, rich beyond all imagination in the power to transform the conditions of its appearance by that energy of prayer which is the vital apprehension of a divine fellowship.

We need also to recognise the boundless complexity of life: the many factors which must contribute to its completeness: the answering blessings of tenderness and reverence: of watchful care and patient trust: of enterprise and waiting: of the love which hopeth all things and the love which beareth all things. We are not placed in the world to essay the vain task of creating humanity afresh. Our part is to learn its capacities, its tendencies, its position, its destiny, and, in the strength and by the light of the Incarnation, to strive unrestingly to bring it a little nearer to its goal. Our aim will be, by the grace of God, not simply to relieve distress but to render relief unnecessary: not to free ourselves from the burden of anxiety by abdicating our heritage, but to use it with thoughtful solicitude for the common weal; to seek to make the conditions of labour for every fellow-man such that he may discharge his office for the family, the nation, the race, and in the effort feel the joy of an accepted sacrifice. II.

We need, yet once more, to embody the ministry of laymen. The order of the Franciscans was characteristically a lay institution. Francis, with his unmeasured devotion, with his missionary zeal, with his gift of preaching, with his love of souls, never received the priesthood. Of the first group of twelve who received the commission to preach from Innocent, one only, as it appears, was in orders. Thus the lesson of the spirit of Francis, the fulfilment of his work, brethren, is for you. His sympathy with every living creature, his feeling for everything without life, as we speak, the hallowing, that is, of all natural science, is for you. The message of peace by which he reconciled the feuds of nobles and towns is for you.

II. The message of purity by which he vindicated the sanctities of home is for you. It is for you, with a clear vision of the will of God, with a sure confidence in the might of God, to lift from the nations the paralysing load which is laid upon them by the ambition and the selfishness of men.

This, I repeat, is your mission, and it is the will of God.

III.

MODERN EFFORTS: THE QUAKERS (GEORGE FOX).

If we live by the Spirit, by the Spirit also let us walk.

GAL. v. 25.

III. *THE QUAKERS.*

LAST Sunday we considered some features in the noblest and most characteristic effort which was made in the middle ages to establish on earth the Kingdom of God. We saw how, when the enthusiasm of chivalrous courage, concentrated in the Crusades, had failed to bring about the glorious vision for which men had looked, that first universal movement of Christendom was followed by the enthusiasm of devoted sacrifice, embodied by Francis of Assisi in his threefold order, which aimed at conquest by absolute self-denial and humility. We saw how for a brief space the spirit which Francis had aroused stirred the soul of the European nations and united princes and beggars in one sacred fellowship of human service. We saw also how that holier Crusade of love failed to complete what it had begun: how it was doomed to failure by the very principles on which it was founded. For it disregarded the inalienable gift of individuality which is the pledge of each man's III.

III. worth in the cause of God. It held of no account the forces of national life through which alone we can reach the full measure of humanity. It concentrated attention, however undesignedly, upon
2 Cor. v. 16. that which is earthly in revelation, on the *Christ after the flesh* rather than on the Risen Lord, and deeply corrupted the purity of the Faith.

So after the death of Francis the long years went on, for God works slowly, and at last in the XVIth century the lessons of the time of discipline which Francis inaugurated were disclosed. Then the peoples stood revealed in their strength. The new had met the old face to face. 'Greece,' in the splendid image of a great interpreter of history, 'had risen from the dead with the New Testament 'in her hand.' A new world had enlarged the thoughts and kindled the hopes of adventurous spirits. A new art had indefinitely multiplied the legions of students and scholars. Manufactures and commerce had received a vast development. The outward unity of Europe, the unity of the Papacy and the Empire, was for ever broken. The sanctity of nations and of men, their separate endowments and responsibilities and duties, I would say rather than their rights, stood out from thenceforth never to be forgotten in the growth and training of the race.

We must take account of these momentous

facts in our view of the progress of the Church. III.
No view of the Reformation can be more superficial than that which regards it simply as negative, as a protest against dominant errors, as a removal of widespread corruptions. It was this, but it was far more than this. It was the affirmation final and decisive, it was, I had almost said, in the order of Providence, the revelation of Individuality, the assertion that every man, every Christian man, has throned in his own heart a sovereign power whose counsel he must seek, seek with unwearied patience, and whose dictates he must obey: that to subject conscience blindly to any external authority is treason: to fail to bring to it every tribute of light and power is moral suicide. No one can rejoice more than I do to maintain that individuality is not the sum of life, but it is an essential part of life in every region of our nature and our work, in our work for the part and for the whole. It is true, though it is not the whole truth, that we must live and die alone, alone with God.

This truth was the positive message of the Reformation, and it has been the distinguishing mark of the later development of Europe, intellectual, social, religious, even where the Reformation has not been formally accepted. The truth has not indeed always been welcomed or

III. guarded. It has not prevailed without grievous defeats and still more perilous exaggerations; but it has prevailed. And in the course of its progress it has influenced the conceptions which men have formed of the Kingdom of God, both in the Roman and in the Reformed Communions. On the one side the Society of Loyola, recognising the infinite varieties of life and character, of place and circumstance, have endeavoured to win from men as they are a partial or a promised homage to the cause which they hold to be divine. On the other side the Society of Friends have declared open war against the fashion of the world, and called each hearer to acknowledge his own immediate obligation to follow the light of God within him. In these opposite endeavours the Jesuits and the Quakers offer the two extreme types of the religious effects of the Renaissance and the Reformation. They both aimed at establishing a Kingdom of God upon earth. They did this in different ways, with different aims, and with different results; and they both failed. It would be of deep interest to trace out the meaning and the moral of the significant contrast which they present. That however I cannot do now. I wish this afternoon to speak of the Quakers only, of their principles and of their work. For the

Quakers appear to me to express with the greatest force and exclusiveness the new thought of the Reformation, the thought of individuality. They give us in a striking form one side of the Gospel, if one side only. And under this aspect their teaching is in many ways a parallel and a complement to that of the Franciscans. III.

Outwardly indeed there was little resemblance between George Fox and Francis of Assisi, between the young Leicestershire shepherd of the XVIIth century and the young Italian merchant of the XIIIth, but they both felt the power of God and yielded themselves wholly to it: both left father and mother and home: both defied the *Journal*, i. pp. 50 ff. opinions of their time: both won their way through bitter opposition to solid success: both cast themselves upon 'the infinite love of God': both were i. pp. 56, 60. most truly 'surrendered' souls; but Francis submitted himself to established authority, Fox only to the Spirit of God speaking in the single soul: Francis saw God in nature and man; Fox looked to God only, and if he sought the woods it was not to commune with nature but to avoid men. He shrank even from the familiar companionship i. p. 50. of friends, lest in this way his sensitiveness to the divine teaching should be impaired.

1. This then is the first point on which I desire to insist. In solitude and silence Fox

III. found God and heard Him. He proclaimed that the Kingdom of God is the Kingdom of a living Spirit Who holds converse with His people. The circumstances of the age called for a bold affirmation of this truth of man's personal converse with God. The upheaval of the Reformation had been followed by innumerable divisions and controversies. Men had lost their sustaining sense of a strong external authority, and they had not learnt the grace of inward self-restraint. They were unwilling to bear for
Luke xxi. 19. a time the reproach of indecision and *win their souls by patience.* They endeavoured to set up some outward standard by the help of which they might enforce submission to their own judgments. On the one side they fashioned an ideal of primitive antiquity to which thought and practice must be conformed: on the other side they relied on the letter of the Bible as capable of a rigid, mechanical application to the problems of a later time. In antagonism to both schools Fox judged truly that the new Protestant scholasticism had not reached to the heart of things in any image of past experience, or in any
i. p. 53. printed Book, however sacred: that academic learning was not in itself an adequate passport to the Christian ministry: that the words of God could not supersede the Word of God. He realised

as few men have ever realised, that we are placed under the dispensation of the Spirit: that the *power from on high* with which the Risen Christ promised to endue His people was no exceptional or transitory gift, but an Eternal Presence, an unfailing spring of energy, answering to new wants and new labours. He felt that the Spirit which had guided the fathers was waiting still to lead forward their children: that He who spoke through men of old was not withdrawn from the world, like the gods of Epicurus, but ready in all ages *to enter into holy souls and make them friends of God and prophets.*

III.

Luke xxiv. 49.

Wisd. vii. 27.

In this conviction Fox himself 'saw' the Truth, Christ Himself shewing it. He gained, that is, the direct assurance that the Gospel is not words, but facts, not a tradition, but a voice even now to the heart of man, which man can recognise and embody in life. He had a vision, partial it may have been but yet distinct, of the *heavens opened and of angels of God ascending and descending upon* redeemed humanity. And others could see that his eyes had looked upon the King. 'The most awful reverent frame I ever saw or felt' writes W. Penn 'was [that of Fox] in prayer[1].'

i. p. 53.

i. p. 64.

Comp. i. p. 61.

John i. 51.

Pref. p. 32; cf. p. 34.

[1] Fox very rarely touches on the larger problems of life; but in one passage of unusual beauty he has told us how the

III. Nor did Fox claim this privilege as something peculiar to himself. Far otherwise. The decisive question which he proposed as a test of the
i. p. 336. vitality of a Church was 'whether it had the Holy Ghost poured forth upon it as the apostles?'

And, brethren, have we not need to put this question to ourselves? Have we not need to ponder heedfully this first lesson of the Society of Friends? We have not to our shame and loss either as a Church, or as living members of a Church, thrown ourselves with strong dependence on Him Whom we confess to be 'Lord' and 'Life-giver.' We seek anxiously, when we desire to move, for patterns and precedents instead of listening in devout silence till the first message to ourselves grows articulate through thoughts opened in many hearts.

2. Here then is the first lesson as to the Kingdom of God which the Society of Friends

last question of our own days was answered for him. 'One
i. p. 65. morning,' he writes, 'as I was sitting by the fire, a great cloud came over me, a temptation beset me; and I sat still. It was said "All things come by Nature"; and the elements and stars came over me, so that I was in a manner quite clouded with it. But as I sat still and said nothing, the people of the house perceived nothing. And as I sat still under it and let it alone, a living hope and a true voice arose in me, which said, "There is a living God, who made all things." Immediately the cloud and temptation vanished away, and life rose over it all; my heart was glad and I praised the living God.'

offers to us. It is a kingdom of spiritual con- III.
verse: and a second is included in it. For Fox maintained that this power of Divine converse belongs to all men by the will of their Creator and Redeemer. He appealed unweariedly without restriction or gloss to the words of St John, in which the Evangelist speaks of '*the light, the true light, which lighteth every man*,' 'a light,' Fox adds, 'sufficient to lead unto the day-star,' because it is a light from God. i. pp. 70, 147, 162, 225, 251, 298 f., 342, &c. i. p. 316.

The importance of this affirmation of the actual affinity of man as man to God, by the divine charter of his constitution, is evident when we recal the character of the current theology of the middle of the XVIIth century. The doctrine of reprobation was then commonly preached with a crude violence which shook the very foundations of morality. In the face of this the message of Fox, given again and again with vigorous simplicity, was the indignant answer of a soul touched by the love of God to human systems, whether of Pelagius or Calvin. And if it was met by the fierce denunciations of technical theologians, it was welcomed as indeed a Gospel by many who 'had not heard the like before.' It opened once again the prospect of that universal kingdom to which Isaiah looked. It gave back to the world the idea of a Divine Fatherhood commensurate

III. with the Divine Love. It offered to the preacher of the good tidings of the Kingdom an assurance sufficient to support his largest hope; for he knew that he could not approach any hearer without having God as his fellow-worker, and the secret voice of the Soul for his witness.

This truth again, necessary when Fox reaffirmed it in the spirit of Greek theology, though he knew not his forerunners, is necessary for the fulfilment of our own work now. We are encouraged by it to use with reverence the apostolic language, and say that the great order of redemption, as it is unfolded to us slowly through
Hebr. ii. 10. the ages, *became God*: to find in the correspondence between the divine method and man's condition a sign of the sovereign authority of revelation more impressive than any possible record of material signs: to know that the Gospel cannot have a stronger attestation than that which may be verified at any moment, even that it is able under the greatest variety of circumstances to fashion believers of every race and every class after the Divine likeness.

3. For there is still a third lesson as to the Kingdom of God flowing from the other two which is declared to us by the Society of Friends. The facts of intercourse with God, of affinity to God, must, if they are received, find expression in life.

The life of believers is, in Christ's own words, the revelation of God to the world. Fox accepted the consequence and insisted upon it. He could not conceive of religion and morality apart. His labours were from first to last a comment on the text, *If we live by the Spirit, by the Spirit let us also walk.* For him justification was indeed a making and not an accounting just, not forensic but loyal; and conduct was the sign of the fact. No one ever required more absolutely than Fox that '*righteousness, peace, joy*' should be the marks of the Christian commonwealth. No one in his personal work more fully realised the truth of the blessing than he did, even through obloquy and persecution and suffering. Four or five hours before his death some friends inquired how he found himself. 'Never heed,' he replied: 'the Lord's power is over all weakness and death: the Seed reigns: blessed be the Lord.' We may think that many of the details on which he laid stress were trivial; but in spite of every infirmity and disproportion, he was able to shape a character in those who followed him which for independence, for truthfulness, for vigour, for courage, for purity, is unsurpassed in the records of Christian endeavour.

III.

ii. 366.

And this he did by connecting the loftiest thoughts and the commonest obligations alike

III. with a personal sense of a divine communion. He made each member of his society responsible for his brethren. He opened to all without distinction the opportunity for spiritual influence: he imposed upon all the charge of social duties. He jealously guarded the sacred dignity of man. No one under his rule could become a 'purchaseable plaything'. And in regard to those without he counselled the Friends no less wisely. He taught them to trust to principles and leave consequences to God: to confess their ideal even when attainment was for the time impossible.

We cannot wonder therefore that the Society of Friends has achieved results wholly out of proportion to their numbers. No religious order can point to services rendered to humanity more unsullied by selfishness or nobler in far-seeing wisdom. Our prisons purified, our criminal law reformed, our punishments rescued at least in part from the dominion of vindictiveness, witness to the success of Quaker labours. Fox was the first who raised his voice against the evils of West Indian slavery, and after 150 years his society was allowed to take a chief part in suppressing it. He claimed freedom for opinion in things pertaining to God, and little by little, through calm and patient endurance, his cause was won. He denounced war, and the doubt, the waste, the threatening, which make an armed peace an almost intolerable burden, must even now be turning the hearts of many to that one experiment of Christian statesmanship which has not yet been tried, the policy of national brotherhood. It may be true, nay, if we hold that man is made in God's image, it must be true, that love is stronger than fear. William Penn was, I believe, the only colonist in America who left his settlement wholly unprotected by fence or arms, and his settlement was the only one which was unassailed by the Indian tribes. III.

These splendid achievements, these significant promises are written in the annals of Quakerism for our strengthening and for our guidance. They have not yet been placed in their harmonious relation to the fulness of Christian life: they have not yet borne their perfect fruit. For though not one of Fox's positive principles can be shewn to have failed, his society has failed. It has not been the seed of the Kingdom of God on earth. It was indeed condemned to failure, like the Order of Francis, because it was essentially incomplete. Francis sacrificed the individual: Fox left wholly out of account the powers of the larger life of the Church and the race. For him the past was 'a long and dismal night of apostasy and darkness'. He had no eye for

III. the *many parts and many fashions* in which God is pleased to work. He had no sense of the action of the Holy Spirit through the great Body of Christ. He had no thought of the weak and immature, for whom earthly signs are the appropriate support of faith: no thought for the students of nature, for whom they are the hallowing of all life. And so it came to pass that he acknowledged no gracious means for the personal appropriation of God's gifts, as he knew no stages in the popular embodiment of the Truth. He disinherited the Christian society, and he maimed the Christian man.

But none the less he established, even more impressively from his false negations, one fundamental fact, which is of momentous importance for us in our present endeavours to bring before the world the majesty of the kingdom of God. He made clear beyond question the power of the simplest spiritual appeal to the consciences of men. He made clear beyond question the efficacy of a childlike trust in the reality of a divine fellowship to cleanse the rudest and coarsest life. For he did not labour towards the accomplishment of any special work of mercy or justice. He strove simply for the recognition of a living Christ within every soul. He wrought for God in the conviction that the new life is the consequence

and not the condition of the quickened Faith;
that *righteousness, peace, joy,* are the notes of the believer but not the prerequisites for believing. He struck, in a word, and he encourages us to strike, at the disease of the sinful, which is ignorance of God, and not at the symptoms of it.

The fact of his success, far-reaching, deep, enduring, is therefore I repeat of momentous importance to us now. We are busied, engrossed, absorbed in dealing with partial evils, with intemperance, with uncleanness, with dishonesty. We think (is it not true?) that we can build up the kingdom of God in fragments; that some breath from heaven will at last animate the frame which we have painfully fashioned bit by bit.

But there is, as far as I can see, little encouragement for such a reversal of the processes of nature, for such a denial of the teaching of history. The principle of life fashions the organism, and sustains it. No organism, however delicately constructed, can summon to itself the principle of life. Men of commanding genius and perfect devotion have devised from time to time schemes of social regeneration, but no scheme has ever shewn a power of continuance which has not been based upon religious faith. No scheme which has retained its first faith has ever wholly failed.

III. *If we live by the Spirit, by the Spirit let us also walk.* That is the law of the Kingdom. That is the law which we have to realise under the conditions of our own age. Next Sunday when the fresh message of the Incarnation has again moved us to believe that *all things are* still *possible*, I hope to suggest some thoughts on the form which our work should take. Meanwhile, brethren, in the prospect of that infinite hope, let us all meditate on St Paul's charge. Let us, while we think of it, bear ourselves as scholars in Christ's school, the school of the living Spirit, the Spirit of Christ, who brings forth from the treasury of heaven things new and old for our use. The Gospel gave to men the eternal truths of equality, freedom, brotherhood, as the basis of our social life, gave them to us in their final shape for men in righteousness, peace, joy; and the Gospel is able to establish them: to establish them with a power which perfects our weakness and a glory which passes our understanding.

IV.

PRESENT PROBLEMS.

[Stephen], being full of the Holy Ghost, looked up steadfastly into heaven, and saw the glory of God and Jesus standing on the right hand of God.

ACTS vii. 55.

(St Stephen's Day.)

IV. *PRESENT PROBLEMS.*

I DESIRE this afternoon to indicate some conclusions which seem to me to follow from the facts which we have been allowed to consider on the last three Sundays. We have seen, you will remember, that the first message of the Gospel was the Advent of the Kingdom of God upon earth, that the message was essentially social and not individual only, that it dealt with the immediate present and not with a remote future. We have seen that the notes of the Kingdom are *righteousness, peace, joy,* in which we found the true interpretation of equality, freedom, brotherhood, as these are embodied in the complex life of men. We have seen that from age to age endeavours have been made to establish the ideal thus offered to hope, which succeeded so far as to reveal the energy of the religious faith by which they were sustained, and which failed so far as to reveal the peril of one-sided developments. We have seen the wide response which was made of old, in

IV. times of sore *distress of nations and perplexity*, to a call for absolute self-sacrifice, for voluntary beggary, and again to an appeal to a divine principle throned in the heart of each man. We have seen that the noblest efforts are doomed to disappointment if they disregard the sacred offices of the individual and of the nation: or if they allow the earthly form of truth to become predominant: or if they cast aside the heritage of the past. We have seen, and this is our final ground of confidence, that spiritual forces are able to quicken and purify the dullest and the coarsest, and to support in healthy vigour the life which they have communicated.

We turn then to the problems of our own age and country, and ask how we can meet them with the help which we may draw from this teaching of earlier experience. In seeking for an answer it is something that there is a general agreement as to the source of our characteristic dangers. We are suffering on all sides, and we know that we are suffering, from a tyrannical individualism. This reveals itself in social life by the pursuit of personal pleasure: in commercial life by the admission of the principle of unlimited competition: in our theories of life by the acceptance of material standards of prosperity and progress. Nor is it difficult to see why this should be so. The silent revolution which has taken place within this century in the methods of production and distribution has terribly intensified the evils which belong to all late forms of civilisation. The 'great industries' have cheapened luxuries and stimulated the passion for them. They have destroyed the human fellowship of craftsman and chief. They have degraded trade, in a large degree, into speculation. They have deprived labour of its thoughtful freedom and turned men into 'hands'. They have given capital a power of dominion and growth perilous above all to its possessor. IV.

So it has come to pass that in our fierce conflicts we are in peril of guiding our conduct by a theory of rights and not by a confession of duties: of losing life in the search for the means of living: of emptying it meanwhile of everything which gives dignity to manhood, though stripped of the accidents of outward dress, and hope to sorrow, though it must be borne in loneliness even to the end. We need therefore in order that we may hold our faith erect in our day of trial to deepen in ourselves the sense of responsibility. We need to shew to the world the reality of spiritual power. We need to gain and to exhibit an idea which satisfies the thoughts, the aspirations, the aims of men straining towards the light.

IV. 1. We need, I say, to deepen in ourselves the sense of responsibility, the sense of responsibility proportioned to our endowments. The first words attributed to man born outside the Paradise of God, are words which disclose the secret of
Gen. iv. 9. all social evil. '*Am I*', said the earliest mur-
Gen. iv. 11, 12. derer, '*my brother's keeper?*' And the answer came from the unfruitful earth, silent witness of the deed of violence; came from the soul, filling with remorse the fugitive who could not flee from himself. Yes: and the same answer must come as often as the thoughtless, the self-indulgent, the idle, propose the question now. We are our brothers' keepers even as they are ours; and unless we accept the charge the scene of our toil and the inexorable sovereign of our hearts will condemn us to unsatisfied desires.

But let us not be mistaken. What we need is a grave sense of responsibility, and not that generous impulsiveness which is swayed this way and that by successive courses of suffering. We cannot with impunity treat the miseries, the crimes, the vices of men, as excitements, spectacles, tragedies, to stir our emotions. They are our grief, our reproach, our shame, because we too are men; and as men we must take them to ourselves. They cry to us with the voice of an awakened conscience, which knows the temptations with which we have dallied and the safeguards by which we have been protected. They bid us ask with persistent resolution till some reply is gained, what means for us that tending of the leper by Francis of Assisi which was for him the revelation of the Lord? What means for us that appeal of George Fox to the drunken rustic which was for him the revelation of *the Light, the true Light which lighteth every man?* IV. John i. 9.

2. We need to quicken our sense of responsibility, and we need also to shew to the world the reality of spiritual forces. This we must do, by the help of God, in forms which correspond with the trials and the temper of the age. Behind every social question there lies not only a moral but also a religious question. And the final solution of every question belongs to the highest sphere. 'You cannot,' in the words of the noblest leader of modern democracy, 'change the 'fate of man by embellishing his material dwelling.' We must touch the soul if we are to change the mode of living. And if we believe that the Gospel teaches us not only to relieve distress but to remove it; not only to alleviate sorrow but to transfigure it; we must make good our faith.

And yet more than this we have a wider duty. Many who allow that Christianity can deal with individuals deny that it has any message for classes or states. Its virtues, they say, are the petty virtues of private life: its promises, the gratification of the small objects of personal aim: towards the struggles of society, of the nation, of the race, it can at the best produce nothing better than a temper of benevolent neutrality. We know that the charge is false, essentially false, but we must admit without reserve that we have given occasion to it. We have not dared, as we should have done, to assert that our Faith in Christ, the Saviour of the world, must be the inspiration of our national policy; that our Faith in the Divine Fatherhood must be the measure of our social obligations. It is not indeed easy to determine in every case the special application of the Truth. It is not necessary that we should determine it; but if we cannot improvise peremptory judgments, we can always affirm an eternal principle: we can quell in our hearts that spirit of self-assertion which fills us with restless jealousy till our personal demands are fully paid, and that spirit of larger, deadlier, self-assertion, miscalled patriotism, which tempts us to think that the power of a nation is the power of dictation and not of service, and that every failure must be washed out in blood. We can do this; and shall we venture to say that we have done it?

3. We need yet once more to gain and to

exhibit a great ideal. We are troubled on the IV.
one side by a spirit of irony which shrinks from the avowal of its loftiest aims; and on the other side by the spirit of confidence which assumes that all will be well if we go with the stream. We play with noble thoughts. Now we want insight, and now we want courage. In both cases we want faith in men, and, that which alone can give it, faith in God. No word is used more familiarly than 'progress', but it is very hard to see the goal towards which we are supposed to be moving. The greatest triumphs of modern science are, as we have seen, fruitful in evils no less than in blessings. They have increased our power, our opportunities, our resources: but in themselves they cannot open the heavens and shew *the glory* Acts vii. 55.
of God and Jesus standing at the right hand of God: they cannot give us that vision of immeasurable majesty which fills the whole soul with the consciousness of its destiny, and that vision of sovereign love which brings the assurance that attainment is within our reach. For we do not think too much of life, too much of humanity, too much of men, but infinitely too little, because we allow that which can be seen by the eye of sense to furnish the data of our estimate. But let us bring the Gospel of Christ, Maker and Heir of all things, into connexion not Hebr. i. 2.

IV. with ourselves only but with the world, and then there will rise before us a spectacle which must move the dullest with enthusiasm and touch the most disconsolate with hope: a spectacle of a life unfolded through the ages in which, in spite of every partial loss and every temporary check, a divine counsel of *righteousness* is fulfilled: of a humanity through whose discipline and victory, won by sacrifice offered in the ministry of every member, the end of the whole creation is reached in the *peace* of an indissoluble harmony: of men who each in their appointed place receive the inheritance of the fathers and transmit it enriched by their own toils to a new generation and
Matt. xxv. 21, 23. enter living and dying into the *joy* of the Lord. What ideal can be offered to the spirit which is greater or more true?

The sense of responsibility, the energy of spiritual force, the power of a divine ideal: how can we gain them? To this question, which is for us the question of all questions, the past returns no uncertain answer. Each new revelation of Christ among men has hitherto found expression in some social movement, in some form of disciplined life which has embodied and interpreted it. And Christ is revealing Himself through the very needs which trouble us. We can see now, as men could not see in earlier times how there has been a law in the growth of the race: how man was taken from himself by the ancient organisations of the state: how he was taken from the world by the dominant religious communities of the middle ages: how he has been taken from society by the isolating narrowness of many forms of popular Protestantism; and seeing this we can see also, when we let the Incarnation give its perfect message, that he is given back to himself, to the world, to society in the Risen Christ. This then is the revelation which we have to embody: to embody in the eyes of all by some fellowship which shall strike the imagination; which shall teach by manifold experience the power of social relationships and social obligations in commerce, in politics, in religion; which shall claim for the family and the nation their proper parts in preparing the Kingdom of God on earth, in bringing to redeemed humanity the fulness of its life in Christ. IV.

I know how utterly unworthy I am to speak of such a fellowship when I look back upon a life of fragmentary efforts and barren convictions, but that which seemed a dream in my own early youth has been I believe brought now within the reach of accomplishment; and among those who hear me may be some whom God is calling to the work of its founding by the thousand voices which in this Abbey bid them take courage from the past.

IV. I do not venture to suggest the rules of the fellowship which I foresee, but I cannot be mistaken as to its main characteristics. The fellowship must be natural. It must not depend for its formation or its permanence on any appeals to morbid or fantastic sentiment. It must accept the facts of life, as seen in the relations of the family, for the ground of its constitution. It must be an attempt not to realise counsels of perfection for a select few, but to give a healthy type of living for all.

The fellowship must be English. The nation is to the race what the family is to the nation. The nation represents on a sufficiently large scale the lessons which are conveyed by God through a common history, a common language, a common home. The nation is an element no less important in the life of the Church than in the life of humanity. And England, alone among the nations, has received the power which is essential for the task which we contemplate, the power of assimilating new ideas without breaking with the past.

The fellowship must be comprehensive. It must deal not with opinion, or feeling, or action only, but with the whole sum of life. It must proclaim that God is not to be found more easily in 'the wilderness and the solitary place' than in the study, or in the market, or in the workshop, or by the fireside. It must banish the strange delusion by which we suppose that things temporal and spiritual can be separated in human action, or that we can render rightly to Cæsar that which is not in the very rendering rendered also to God. IV.

The fellowship must be social. Every member of it must hold himself pledged to regard his endowments of character, of power, of place, of wealth, as a trust to be administered with resolute and conscious purpose for the good of men: pledged to spread and deepen the sense of one life, one interest, one hope, one end for all, in the household, in the factory, in the warehouse, in the council-room: pledged to strive as he has the opportunity to bring all things that are great and pure and beautiful within the reach of every fellow-worker: pledged to labour so that to the full extent of his example and his influence toil may be universally honoured as service to the state, literature may be ennobled as the spring and not the substitute of thought, art (too often the minister of luxury) may be hallowed as the interpreter of the outward signs of God's working.

The fellowship must be open. The uniform of the soldier is at once a symbol and a safe-

IV. guard. It reminds others of his obligations, and supports him in the endeavour to fulfil them. It makes some grave faults practically impossible. So too a measured and unostentatious simplicity, a simplicity in dress, in life, in establishment, widely adopted by choice and not of necessity, will be an impressive outward witness to the Christian ideal, and it will help towards the attainment of it.

The fellowship must be rational. It must welcome light from every quarter, as found by those who know that every luminous ray, reflected or refracted a hundred times, comes finally from one source. It must make it clear that Christians as Christians strive not for victory but for truth, that they, of all men, are least willing to satisfy the soul by mutilating its capacities, or deadening its sensibility.

The fellowship above all must be spiritual. It must rest avowedly on the belief that the voice of God is not silent among us, and the vision of God not withdrawn from His people. It must labour in the assurance that the difference of our age from the first age is not the difference of the dull, dim twilight from the noon, but that of common earth, flooded with sunshine, from the solitary mountain-top kindled to a lamp of dawn. It must find occasion for continual praise and thanksgiving in victories of faith, from that of the first martyr St Stephen to that of the last boy in U-Ganda who knew at least how to die for his Saviour. It must not weary of proclaiming that we—we poor, frail, erring creatures—*live and move and have our being* in God, and that we are surrounded by sacraments of His Presence and of His grace. It must summon its followers not in the name of well-being and happiness but in the name of duty and love, made known to us in their scope and their efficacy by the Birth and the Passion of Christ. It must bring home to each noblest and each meanest that he—he in his great estate, he in his utter desolation—is a temple, a priest, a sacrifice to a living God.

IV.

Acts xvii. 28.

Such a fellowship of 'brethren and sisters of the common hope' may seem to some to be visionary: to others, I think, it will be only the expression of their own deep longings. It is at least, as far as I can judge, nothing more than the translation of our Creed into action according to the conditions of the time. The way to the new and fuller life must still be, as it always has been, through heaven.

And if it seem visionary, I can only say that I have suggested nothing which has not been realised on a large scale, under harder circumstances and with scantier knowledge than our own by Franciscans, by Moravians, by Quakers. Those Societies were not disciplined by that discernment of the laws of national and human growth which has been given to our later years. They were not supported by that catholic sympathy with every energy of man which has been quickened among us by a large interpretation of nature and history. We have learnt what they could not know. The counsel of God for humanity has been made clear to us not only in its general character, but also in the mode of its fulfilment. We can estimate fairly the resources of the race. No dark continents, no untried peoples, fill the dim background of our picture of the world with incalculable possibilities. The whole field lies before us. We look upon all the provinces of the kingdom of God. We can communicate to others the noblest which we have and save them from the long pains of our discipline. All things are ready.

All things are ready: and to you, my younger brethren, the charge is first offered of claiming the final victory for Christ. The issue will, I believe, if we may trust the cycles of the past, be decided in your generation. Look backward, then, for the inspiring encouragement of Christian experience. Look forward for the glorious assurance of Christian hope. But look around you, without closing your ears to one bitter cry, or closing your eyes against one piteous sight, or refusing thought to one stern problem, for your proper work, and thankfully accept it in the name of God. IV.

Whether you are moved by the Holy Spirit, sent in Christ's Name, to form for yourselves some fellowship such as I have indicated or not, live at any rate, however hard it is, as Christians, as citizens of that Kingdom of which the notes are *righteousness, peace, joy.* Confess gladly that the Gospel has not only strong consolation for those whose work is well-nigh over but, even more essentially, inspiration for those whose work is yet to be done. Let nothing rob you of the conviction that the voice of God can be heard, and is heard '*To-day*': that the vision of God can be gained, and is gained, '*To-day*'. Keep the eyes of your heart fixed, not for the present on the Christ pierced and bleeding on the tree, but on the Risen Christ, reigning on the Father's throne. Look upward, eager to live, ready to die, for Him; and you too, like St Stephen, will see *the heavens opened,*—see the communion of the visible and the invisible reestablished,—you will see *the glory of God,*—see a fresh manifestation of His purifying, quickening love,—you will see *Jesus the*

Hebr. iii. 13.

IV. *Son of man,* the Creator and Heir of all things, *standing at the right hand of God,* risen from His royal seat to support and welcome each baffled and fainting servant.

Mark x. 51, 52. *Jesus...said, What wilt thou that I should do unto thee? And the blind man said unto Him, Rabboni, that I may receive my sight. And Jesus said unto him, Go thy way; thy faith hath made thee whole. And straightway he received his sight and followed Him on the way.*

May God grant to us all the power of vision and the grace of sacrifice, in the light of Christmas, and in the life of the Incarnate Son of God.

APPENDIX.

TYPES OF APOSTOLIC SERVICE.

I. *Saintship.*
II. *Authority.*
III. *Suffering:* ST PAUL.
IV. *Doubting:* ST THOMAS.
V. *Waiting:* ST JOHN.

We are come to...the heavenly Jerusalem and to innumerable hosts of angels...and the church of the firstborn enrolled in heaven....

HEB. xii.

St Bartholomew's Day, 1885.

I. *SAINTSHIP.*

WE were led to consider yesterday some aspects of the great spiritual fellowship to which we have been introduced by the Risen Lord, of the common service rendered to God by the *innumerable hosts of angels* and *the church of the firstborn,* our unseen fellow-soldiers in heaven and our unrecognised fellow-soldiers on earth. To-day the thought receives a special shape. The commemoration of Saints is one of the provisions which has been wisely made by our Church to bring home to us our connexion with the invisible life: to help us to confess that they who once lived to God live still; to know that we are heirs not of a dead past, but of a past fresh with new lessons; to learn that consecrated gifts become an eternal blessing; to understand—most touching mystery—that Christ is pleased to reveal Himself little by little, *in many parts and in many fashions* in the persons of His servants.

APPEND. I.

Thus it is that each saint receives and shews some trait of the perfect Manhood of his Master. And 'we that are but parts' can recognise on a scale suited to our weakness now this grace and now that according to our needs. Thus it is that slowly and through manifold energies the members shew us the grandeur and beauty of the One life by which they are inspired: that we come to feel that there is a place for us also in the vast Temple which is reared through the ages on the Foundation of Christ for the glory of God.

It is therefore of deep interest to strive to seize the individuality of the Saint whom we commemorate; and there is much in the brief notices of Bartholomew—Nathanael—whom we commemorate to-day on which I might dwell. But I wish now (in the few minutes which are allowed me) to speak more generally. I wish, if I may, to bring the thought of Saintship a little nearer to us.

And first let me ask you to remember that the mark of a saint is not perfection but consecration. A saint is not a man without faults, but a man who has given himself without reserve to God. In the language of the New Testament every baptized Christian—dead and buried and raised in Christ—is a saint. We are dwelling among saints: we are saints. That is the will of God for us. If it is unaccomplished, the failure comes through our faithlessness.

It follows that in the narrower sense of the word the age of saints is not past. There has never been a time when the Gospel has not vindicated its sovereignty and Christ has not found His living interpreters. We have not as yet been taught to give an open place in our public services to the later heroes of faith, but I trust nevertheless that they are not forgotten. I trust that we call up in grateful memory saints whom we have known—the glory of their devoted service—to give distinctness to thanksgiving and hymn. There is not one among us whose study and whose experience may not bring some dear companion, whom he has learnt to recognise in the silent converse of books or in the stirring conflicts of duty, to swell 'the glorious company 'of the Apostles,' and 'the goodly fellowship of 'the prophets,' and 'the noble army of martyrs,' men who in these later days and in our own Church have heard a call of God and have obeyed it, men who have seen a truth of God and have interpreted it, men who have received a burden at the hands of God and in trust on Him have borne it, saints who have not been reckoned in any calendar.

APPEND. I. Such thoughts are natural everywhere, but in this Abbey they are even necessary. It has been called 'a temple of silence and reconciliation'. It is far more truly an altar of human endowments. Here is laid the memorial of every form of true service which men have rendered to God out of His manifold fulness. Here the world is offered for our meditation as it is in His sight. Here that lives which was given to Him, lives and works still, purified from every admixture of earthly selfishness. And if, as we heard this morning, the patriarch, when his eyes were opened saw in the bare wilderness *the house of God* and *the gate of heaven*, shall not we find helps about us here to see *Him who is invisible?*

Gen. xxviii. 17. Hebr. xi.

And in the Abbey this Chapel [of Henry VII.] has its own peculiar message. It is as it were, the tomb, the monument, of mediævalism. Designed to be the shrine of a canonised king it became the resting-place of three dynasties separated outwardly by sharp differences from his Communion.

In both relations it speaks to us something of the nature of the eternal and the unseen. It speaks to us in the long line of statues which encircle it—unique in England,—in which for the last time the middle age expressed its faith in the great communion of saints. It speaks to us in the costly structures and plain stones of later times which cover the dust of those to whom for a brief space earthly empire was committed. APPEND. I.

We can hardly look upon that long line supported by the cornices of angels without feeling the conviction which it expresses of the manifoldness of consecrated service. Philosophers, kings, priests, warriors, doctors, apostles, holy maids and matrons, lead up to the central figure of the enthroned Lord, blessing the world which He rules.

We can hardly look upon the strange contrast of splendour and bareness in the royal graves without feeling that the soul is not measured by 'glory of birth and state'. Nowhere can the famous words of one whose last public act was performed here before long years of romantic tragedy find a richer commentary: 'O eloquent, just and 'mighty Death! whom none could advise thou 'hast persuaded: what none have dared thou hast 'done: and whom all the world hath flattered 'thou only hast cast out of the world and de-'spised: thou hast drawn together all the far-'stretched greatness, all the pride, cruelty and 'ambition of men and covered it all over with 'these two narrow words: *Hic jacet.*'

And so it is that the tomb often speaks with a power of revelation. There is a sad pathos even in the words of idle praises which seek to carry

APPEND. I. into another order the conventional forms of this. But there are also true voices which come to us with a secret and irresistible force and open the secret of that which is in the words of our Founder 'the land of the living'.

Let me remind you of three voices which must ever speak to us in this Chapel, three voices from three centuries, which, I think, come from the heart and reach the heart.

On the monument beneath which lie the two Tudor Queens, inevitably divided by birth, by fortune, by faith, we read:

> Regno consortes et urna hic obdormimus Elizabetha et Maria sorores in spe resurrectionis.

Buckingham [Sheffield], statesman, soldier, poet, seems to describe the unsatisfied spirit of his time when he closes the half-faltering confession of doubt with a prayer of penitence:

> Dubius sed non improbus vixi:
> Incertus morior, non perturbatus.
> Humanum est nescire et errare.
> Deo confido
> Omnipotenti, benevolentissimo.
> Ens entium miserere mei.

And on the latest slab which covers those whom we ourselves were allowed to see 'uniting 'many hearts from many lands and drawing all to 'things above', the words of St John are a fresh testimony of experience:

We know that we have passed from death unto life because we love the brethren. APPEND. I.

The blessing of saintship in the final victory over every difference of earth: the foundation of saintship in the cry of absolute self-surrender to an Almighty Sovereign: the activity of saintship in services of tender ministry: do we not know that the voices are for us?

Consecration, as I said, and not perfection is the mark of the Saint. We have all that which we can offer to God: we have all that which God is pleased to seek. *We are come to the heavenly Jerusalem, and to innumerable hosts of angels and to the Church of the firstborn.* Hebr. xii. 22.

Therefore let us also, seeing we are compassed about with so great a cloud of witnesses...run with patience the race that is set before us, looking unto Jesus the author and perfecter of faith. Hebr. xii. 1 f.

II.

AUTHORITY.

The kings of the Gentiles have lordship over them; and they that have authority over them are called Benefactors. But ye shall not be so; but he that is the greater among you, let him become as the younger; and he that is chief, as he that doth serve.

St Luke xxii. 25 f.

St Bartholomew's Day, 1886.

II. *AUTHORITY.*

THESE words from the Gospel of the day indicate a fundamental difference between heathen and Christian morality. On the one side there is the supreme authority of force: on the other side the supreme authority of service. The force may be intellectual or physical, but he that exercises it provides that his superiority shall be felt and acknowledged. The service may be rendered by one who has the unquestioned prerogative of years or place—by one who is older or by one who is called to lead—but he who renders it merges every claim to preeminence in the unaffected naturalness of his ministry. In the one case the individual himself asserts and claims homage as he stands alone: in the other case the body enjoys the vital office of the member, and the joy of the member is the consciousness of the common life. APPEND. II.

The conception of life which is expressed in this contrast is characteristic of our Faith. It is the glory of Christianity that it has given dignity

APPEND. II. to weakness. The first beatitude—*Blessed are the poor*—is indeed a moral Gospel: the truth which the Life and Work of Christ has made intelligible and attainable. Yes: we dare to say *Blessed are the poor, the poor in spirit,* not the poor-spirited, but they who in their inmost souls recognise the nobility of those traits which we habitually connect with the poor, the sense of reverence, the necessity of labour, the condition of dependence, the continuity of service. Reverence, labour, dependence, service, these are marks of that social life which is founded in Christ, and which draws from Him its benediction and its strength.

But here let us not be mistaken. In hallowing this ideal Christianity has not lowered the standard of human dignity. It has raised the standard immeasurably, while it has shewn that the highest is within the reach of all. It has opened our eyes to see a glory on the earth, a divine Presence everywhere about us, while it has written the sentence of transitoriness and corruption over all the objects of sense. It has emphasised the obligation of toil, while it has shewn that its painfulness is due to the disorder of our nature. It has revealed the reality of the one life by which we all live and to which we can all contribute, while it has made clear that isolation, the proud self-containment of the soul which dwells alone, is death. It has disclosed the true secret of power while it has defined the manner of its exercise.

In the light of the Gospel (to sum up all), and, may I not say, in the deep consciousness of the heart which it illuminates, reverence is the acknowledgment of a transforming grace, labour is the glad return for healthy vigour, dependence is the joy of fellowship, service is the secret of prevailing authority.

This whole ideal is absolutely fulfilled and exhibited and vindicated in the Person of Christ; and so specially is the last thought, that of the authority of service, which is brought before us to-day; *He that is the greater among you*, the Lord says, *let him become as the younger; and he that is chief as he that doth serve;* and then He enforces the command, as you will notice, by His own action, for He continues: *I am in the midst of you, as he that doth serve.*

This is indeed the meaning for us—the essential meaning—of the example of the Lord. The example of Christ, so far as it is proposed for our imitation, is always the example of patience, of self-surrender, of serving, of suffering. The voice which calms and strengthens us is that voice of prevailing love which establishes its power on

APPEND. II. tenderness, and its right to teach on humility. *Take My yoke upon you, and learn of Me*, Christ said—not because I am irresistible with the plenitude of divine might; not because I am omniscient with the fulness of divine vision, but—*because I am meek and lowly in heart, and ye shall find rest unto your souls.*

Matt. xi. 29.

This teaching was strange to those who first heard it. It is not surprising therefore that it should have been repeated again and again like the corresponding revelation of life through death. Each of the first three Evangelists records the substance of the text as spoken twice; and from a comparison of their narratives we can distinguish three occasions, all in the latest stage of the Lord's ministry, when He pressed upon His disciples the authority of service, once immediately after the Transfiguration, again on the last journey to Jerusalem, and a third time in the Holy City. On each occasion the circumstances naturally gave rise to the hope of an immediate outward triumph, the hope of sovereignty for the Lord and of honours for His followers. On each occasion the prospect of success stirred in the twelve thoughts of ambition and rivalry. On each occasion the Lord's words make clear beyond doubt that the blessing of power is 'the blessing of great cares,' that the sign of authority is the readiness to serve.

Luke ix. 46 ff. Matt. xx. 25 ff. Luke xxii. 25 ff.

The lesson was strange, I said, when it was first given, and if we have now grown familiar with its form we can hardly claim to have mastered its spirit. But none the less when we calmly look on the face of things we shall see that the principle of the authority of service is universally true. It is true in regard to nature, to society, to self; it is proved true by the power of insight, of sympathy, of freedom which springs from service. And in spite of our habitual unwillingness to follow the judgements of our hearts we ourselves gladly acknowledge its truth. In the region of thought our highest praise is given to the devotion of patient study: in the region of action to the devotion of self-forgetful labour.

1. The principle is true, I repeat, in regard to Nature. It is an old maxim that we can rule Nature only by obeying her. And exact knowledge is the first requisite for right obedience, a knowledge not of the superficial phenomena, of the appearances of things, but of the laws which the phenomena half hide and half reveal. Such knowledge comes only through watchful, self-repressing search. He who carries his own prejudices and prepossessions to the inquiry into physical truth will certainly find them confirmed. For there is a strange irony in Nature. She speaks in parables; and we must yield ourselves

APPEND. II. to her spirit before we can apprehend their meaning If we are self-willed or hasty or confident, still more if we are imperious or arrogant, she will betray us, though she 'never did betray the soul that loved her'. But that condition is indispensable. Her disguises, her seeming contradictions, are only to be resolved by the loving patience of an unwearied ministry. Insight which is the inspiration of science comes from service.

2. So it is in regard to Government. The true ruler is not he who enforces his will by the bayonets of strong battalions, but he who divines the worthiest desires of his people and claims their homage by shewing that he has entered into their hearts. It lies in our nature that we should respond to the voice which interprets us to ourselves. We cannot but rejoice to obey him who proposes to us that ideal as our own which often we have not the courage to confess, though we inwardly strive towards it. Christ Himself confirms the law in its widest application. He shews that His sovereignty is established on His individual knowledge of His
John x. 3. servants. *He calleth His own sheep by name and* then, not till then, not till He has realised this personal relationship, *He leadeth them out.* His many sheep are not to Him a mere flock. His eye discerns in each that which modifies the

common features. For us such individual knowledge can only be gained by the most reverent and untiring observation. We must serve in order that we may understand. We must not overpower by our own force the character which we wish to appreciate and guide in its mature vigour. He is no true leader who drills his subjects into mechanical instruments of his designs. The true leader gains the devotion of the soul and the spirit. Sympathy, which is the strength of government, comes by service. APPEND. II.

3. The same principle holds good in our personal discipline. It is by serving that we learn the value and the proportion of our own endowments. The consciousness of a divine presence about us, issuing in continual worship, sustains us under the pressure of distracting anxieties. Out of this rises the spirit of reverence, which becomes the perennial source of self-respect by moving us to a thousand little acts of dutiful attention. For such offices of thoughtful ministry do not abase but exalt us. Christian service is indeed a germ of new power. It is not the inconsiderate scattering of our gifts, but the deliberate bestowal of them in such a way that we *may take them again.* If the terrible saying of John x. 17.
the Roman historian is true that 'it is characteristic of human nature that we should hate those whom we have injured,' it is no less true that we love

APPEND. II. those whom we have helped. In this way then by serving God in man and man in God we bring ourselves into harmony with all about us. We ascertain the limits of our ability and the right direction of our work. We gain the fulness of our own nature and bring ourselves into obedience to its laws. We become, that is, free in the true sense of the word, untroubled by the waywardness of caprice and the gusts of restless ambition. Freedom which is the soul of individual life comes through service.

In every direction the authority of service is seen to be supreme. To find the purpose of God about us, in the world and in men, and to offer ourselves without reserve for its accomplishment, that is the rule of Christ, which He will enable us to obey: that is the measure of the authority which He designs us to exercise in the divine order. And it is a rule for all, a rule of infinite peace and of infinite gladness.

That is the secret of keeping the temporal greatness which may have been given to some of us; of winning the eternal greatness which is designed for all of us by God's love. Its blessings do not depend upon power or opportunity. They are for each one according to the use which he makes of the little or much which is committed
Luke x. 30. to him. *There are last,* so it is written, *which shall be first, and there are first which shall be last.*

III.

SUFFERING. (St Paul.)

I (ἐγώ) *will shew him how many things he must suffer for My name's sake.*

Acts ix. 16.

St Paul's Day, 1886.

III. *SUFFERING.*

THE Festival of St Paul which we celebrate to-day differs in a most significant manner from the other Festivals of Saints. It commemorates his conversion and not his martyrdom, the beginning and not the close of his earthly ministry; his spiritual birth, if I may so speak, into this age, and not his birth into the age to come. APPEND. III.

The reason of the difference is not far to seek. The work of St Paul is brought before us with exceptional fulness in the New Testament. He is shewn to be the founder of the Gentile Churches, the teacher who, in the Providence of God, more than any other, has impressed his own character on the Faith which we have inherited. In him the transition from the persecutor to the apostle was outwardly most sudden and startling. We naturally therefore dwell upon his labours as they flowed from 'his marvellous conversion,' on his conversion as the spring of an influence to which history can shew no parallel.

APPEND. III.

Under this aspect to-day's Festival completes the triad of thoughts which the Festivals of this month have offered for our consideration. On New Year's Day we welcomed the general thought of 'the dedication of life,' the dedication through suffering. On the Epiphany this common lesson was brought home to us by the special thought of 'offerings' in which we bring to God the choicest firstfruits of that which He has given to each one of us. And now the thought of offerings is consummated in the thought of 'ser-'vice.' We are encouraged by the example of St Paul to render to the Lord not only what we have but what we are, not our endowments only but ourselves.

The words which I have taken for a text present the thought in an unexpected form. They give us the Lord's view of service; and His view is not as our view. They speak not of achievements, of successes, of long efforts crowned by triumph, but simply of sufferings. The greatness of the accompanying suffering is the one feature which the Ascended Saviour emphasises in the testimony which His new witness is to bear. He overcomes the misgivings of the alarmed disciple, who shrank from receiving the unexpected and suspicious convert with the assurance *He is a chosen vessel unto Me......for I will shew him how*

APPEND. III.

many things he must suffer for My Name's sake.' He does not say, 'I will shew him how many 'thing he will dare and do and win: how many 'things he will learn and teach: how he will bear 'My Gospel to the borders of the West: how he 'will vindicate the spiritual freedom of believers: 'how he will present to the eyes of men the 'vision of a Church as broad as humanity:' but simply this, '*I will shew him how many things* '*he must suffer.*' This is his service: to bear the cruelties which he had before inflicted: to offer himself as a victim even as he had before *made havoc of the Church:* to endure the punishment of St Stephen, and fulfil the first martyr's interrupted work. And we can all feel that this is the true measure of the essence of the Christian life. What we can do for another is the test of power: what we can suffer for another is the test of love. Acts viii. 3.

I will shew him how many things he must suffer. There is a pathos in the original which is almost necessarily lost in the English rendering. In the original the emphasis falls upon the first pronoun. '*I will shew him:*' 'I myself 'will reveal to him My counsel: I will make 'known to him the secret of My victory: I who 'have suffered for him and for all men will 'strengthen him to bear his cross after Me. This

APPEND. III. 'shall be the seal of his commission. This shall be 'the sign of his election. He shall bear, though 'it is a heavy burden (βαστάσει), the message of 'a Saviour Born, Crucified, Ascended, before scorn- 'ful Gentiles and unbelieving Jews. Not one 'grief shall come upon him as an unwelcome 'surprise or a barren trial. *For I will shew him* '*how many things he must suffer for My Name's* '*sake.*

The destiny was foretold and we all know how it was accomplished. St Paul has left us a summary of his sufferings during the first two-thirds of his ministry. (2 Cor. xi. 24 ff.) *Of the Jews five times received I forty stripes save one. Thrice was I beaten with rods, once was I stoned, thrice I suffered shipwreck, a night and a day have I been in the deep......Besides those things that are without, there is that which presseth upon me daily, anxiety for all the churches.* By such discipline he had already learnt to (2 Cor. xi. 30.) *glory—if he needs must glory—of the things that concerned his weakness.* But perhaps we hardly realise how large a part that which appeared to be failure and which was pain had in the fulfilment of his Mission. And in saying this, I am not thinking of the effect which disappointment and sorrow have in purifying and strengthening personal character, but of their outward results.

To take one illustration only. Most of the letters of St Paul through which he speaks with a living voice to all ages were called out by distressing anxieties, or written from confinement. The Epistles to the Thessalonians were due to an exceeding desire to learn something of the state of the Church from which he had been suddenly hurried away, when *once and again Satan had hindered him* from visiting them. The Corinthians by their divisions and their disorders, no less than by their questions, drew from him the portraiture of love and the apostolic statement of the Gospel of the Resurrection. The apostasy of the Galatians stirred him to a burning denunciation of legal righteousness. Even the studied exposition of the Faith addressed to the Romans was due in part to the frustration of his purpose to visit them. As a prisoner first at Cæsarea and then at Rome he might seem to have been kept from the true sphere of his energy, and it is to that period of calm labour that we owe the fuller views of the Person of the Lord and the larger conception of the Church which are given in the Epistles of the Captivity.

APPEND. III.

1 Thess. ii. 18.

Rom. i. 13.

Everywhere there is the same witness. We can see, to use St Paul's own words, how *the things which happened unto him*—the things which overthrew his cherished designs and con-

Phil. i. 12.

APPEND. III. demned him to bear and to wait—*fell out rather unto the progress of the Gospel.* We can see how his service was in those parts in which it proved most fruitful, the service of suffering.

The service of suffering: St Paul learnt the lesson, and to-day he offers it to us. It is a paradox of faith which we find it hard to learn. We would do some great thing and God, by an unlooked-for change of health or fortune or position, forces us to sit still. So His will is accomplished; and in due time we find that our true end also is gained. Our robes are *washed and made white—in blood.* Apoc. vii. 14.

The service of suffering: by this God equalises our circumstances. All are on a level of advantage in respect to this ministry. All can accept the place of patient learners in the school of affliction; and more things are wrought by quiet, uncomplaining, endurance than the world knows of. For a time the eloquence of adversity meekly borne may be unheard, but when it is heard it prevails.

The service of suffering: it is the comprehensive fulfilment of the Lord's promise, *Whosoever shall lose his life for My sake shall find it.* Matt. xvi. 25. It gives to us all in simple ways, in the accomplishment of our common work, in looking calmly, it may be, upon insoluble problems, in surrendering our will to the claims of social duty, the opportunity of gaining the true life.

The service of suffering: it is the revelation of peace. The man of restless ambition undergoes a thousand martyrdoms. But the trials which are accepted as God's gift, to be borne for His name's sake, are transformed by the acceptance. Thus they become a double blessing: a blessing to those who regard them from without as a manifest sign of the Divine Presence with such as endure: a blessing to those who sustain them as an occasion for fresh victories of faith.

IV.

DOUBTING. (St Thomas.)

Then saith He to Thomas, Reach hither thy finger and see My hands; and reach hither thy hand, and put it into My side; and be not faithless but believing.

St John xx. 27.

St Thomas's Day, 1886.

IV. *DOUBTING.*

THERE is nothing which strikes the student of the Gospels more deeply than the revelation which they give of the personal insight and tenderness of the Lord. This is especially true of the Gospel of St John. The Evangelist whom Jesus loved, who lay upon His bosom, knew, if we may so speak, His Master's heart. The love which he received quickened with a keener intelligence the love which he felt.

So it is that we can see in St John's narrative how Christ graciously trained His Apostles; how He bore with them, guided them, disciplined them; how at one time He answered them, and at another time committed them to the silent teaching of life and the solemn exercise of patient, unsatisfied expectation; how He used even their weaknesses and failings for the fuller manifestation of His truth. In no case is this divine method of education shewn more impressively or more instructively than in the case of St Thomas, whom we commemorate to-day. In the other

APPEND. IV. Gospels St Thomas is a name and nothing more: in St John he is a living man, hampered by human infirmities and ennobled by human devotion, a living man, nearer perhaps to ourselves, in our day of trial, than any other of the disciples. St Thomas felt and expressed difficulties by which we are perplexed, and Christ Himself dealt with them. St Thomas doubted, and through his experience we can learn the legitimate issues of doubt. He doubted, in the words of Augustine, which find a place in our own Collect, that we may not doubt, or rather doubt only that we may come to a higher faith. Only four utterances of St Thomas have been recorded and these, as I said, only by St John. They all belong to the last few weeks of the Lord's ministry; but they are sufficient to make the Apostle known. He had followed the Lord during His public work. He had seen His signs, and heard His words, and lived in His presence; and now at the last the thoughts of his heart are revealed. I desire therefore to recal the history that we may meditate upon it. It has, I think, a message for us.

The first occasion on which St Thomas appears John xi. is when the tidings came from Bethany, *Behold, he whom Thou lovest is sick*, which determined the Lord to return to Judæa and place Himself once more in the power of His deadly enemies. *After* two days *He saith: Let us go into Judæa again.* There was but one thought among the disciples: *They said, Rabbi, the Jews were but now seeking to stone Thee; and goest Thou thither again?* Their fear was perfectly well-founded. The Lord did not set it aside. The journey was unto death for Himself, but it was unto life for Lazarus, and unto faith for them. So He definitely invited them a second time to share His peril and visit the friend whom they had lost who was still their friend: *let us go to him.* We can picture the still sadness which fell upon the little band when they heard the words. At last the silence was broken; broken not by St Peter, dauntless in impetuous courage, not by St John, strong in unquestioning love, but by St Thomas. *Thomas said unto his fellow-disciples, Let us also go that we may die with Him.* He who perhaps believed least was most prompt to act on what he did believe. He accepted the invitation and what he thought must be the consequence. He saw only a little way, but he saw clearly. He shrank from buoying himself up with illusions. He did not even dwell upon the mysterious result which the Lord connected with the journey. It was—so much was sure—a journey to death: as such he would share it. He could die for the Lord whom he had known, though (or should I say because?) he

APPEND. IV. could not affect a faith which he had not reached. Ignorance as to the real scope and meaning of the Lord's words left absolute self-sacrifice possible. And we must observe that the sacrifice was accepted. No explanation, as far as we know, was given by the Lord to relieve the dark forebodings of His apostles. They went with Him, Thomas leading, ready to die with Him.

Doubt as to personal consequences is no bar to the power of devotion.

So the journey was taken. At once Lazarus was called back from the grave. In one sense death was overcome; and the enthusiasm of the multitude checked for a moment the designs of chief priests and Pharisees. The immediate fear of the twelve therefore was unfulfilled. As the fear passed away there must have come to them in place of it strange, vague, hopes of a kingdom to be established for Israel, of princely judgment-thrones, of some glorious triumph. But with these hopes other thoughts also were mingled. The disciples could not fail to see that the hostility of the Jewish leaders was only biding its time. They could not fail to notice the warnings of terrible and unexpected sufferings which the Master uttered. Then came the eve of the Passover, and while the hearts of all were burning with the memories of the Old Covenant, with the dim anticipations of the New, the Lord spoke to them of His departure, even as He had spoken to the Jews, *Whither I go ye cannot come.* Such departure was still more perplexing than death. They could die with Him: why could they not follow Him? The prophecy of denial by the boldest was the sufficient answer. But consolation followed. *I go,* Christ said, *to prepare a place for you...And whither I go ye know the way.* However dimly even Apostles might realise the goal of the Lord's labours, they could at least see the direction in which He was moving. Still there was room for questioning; and Thomas frames the question. *Thomas saith unto Him, Lord we know not whither Thou goest; how know we the way?* The difficulty which is thus raised is a real and a natural one. It is true in common life that the knowledge of the end enables us to judge of the road. But it is not so in spiritual things. There the end belongs to another order. It lies beyond our power of distinct apprehension. It is enough therefore for us to know the road, as it is opened to us step by step. And here fresh light is given. Christ shews that for us the end and the road are one. '*I am,*' He says—'I am' and not 'I reveal' or 'I point to' as herald or prophet—'*the Way and the Truth and the Life.*' He meets St Thomas's difficulty by

APPEND. IV.

John xiii. 33.

John xiv. 2 ff.

John xiv. 6.

APPEND. IV. fixing his attention upon Himself. He leads him to see that ignorance as to the future and the unseen can be borne when we are able to appeal to present love and present experience.

Doubt as to the end is no reason for refusing to move along the opened way.

The scenes of the betrayal, the judgment, the Passion swiftly followed. Death came to the Lord in a form more terrible than could have been foreseen, the death of a slave amidst the mockery of priests and people. What then re-
Luke xxiv. 19 ff. mained to those who had hoped that the prophet of Nazareth should have redeemed Israel? What remained? The answer was still, Christ Himself remained, transfigured and yet the same. When the desolate company were gathered together on the third day in fear and yet, as we must believe, with some uncertain recollection of sayings unheeded at the time, but made clearer through
John xx. 19 ff. sorrow, *Jesus came and stood in the midst* and spoke to them the double message of peace. *But Thomas was not with them.* He did not (as it seems) share the hope with which the others were assembled. He must wait for fuller knowledge; and when they told their tidings *he said to them, Except I shall see in His hands the print of the nails and put my finger into the print of the nails*

and put my hand into His side, I will not believe. APPEND. IV.
He fashioned for himself a test of the reality of the Resurrection. Nothing short of this could (he thought) satisfy him, and even this might fail. The death he had seen was too real, the gaping wounds which he recalled were too terrible, to be reconciled with thoughts of life by mere hearsay. He frankly and sadly confessed what was in his heart; and then he endured without losing all hope the long, dreary, days of waiting which followed. For after a full week we read *again* John xx. 26 ff.
the disciples were within and Thomas with them. He had not left their company though he had not shared their joy: they had not disowned him though his faith was clouded. *Then Jesus cometh,... and said Peace be unto you. Then saith He to Thomas Reach hither thy finger and see My hands; and reach hither thy hand, and put it into My side; and be not faithless but believing.* Christ then though unseen had heard the words which Thomas had spoken when he was doubting of His Resurrection, and He offered the test which had been required. But in that most loving Presence, realised by the heart if through the eye, Thomas rose at once beyond every conclusion which the senses could establish. He spontaneously declared the utter impotence of the criterion which he had chosen to determine the truth which he

APPEND. IV. grasped at length. He recognised the Lord, living again, the Lord whom he had followed in trustful discipleship. So much hand and eye might have established if earthly life—life doomed to death—were all. But St Thomas now recognised far more than this life, and this life itself in a higher form. Sight, hearing, touch, were, he now knew, only occasions and starting-points of faith. At one bound—at one bound because he had calmly measured the depths of death—he reached a height of conviction which none had attained before: *he answered and said unto Him, My Lord and my God.*

Doubt as to the validity of historic evidence is no obstacle to the victory of faith.

The sublime confession of St Thomas—a confession won through the doubt which clung to love rather than to life, the doubt which was content, though darkness was before, to tread in the steps of Him who was known, the doubt which acknowledged the powerlessness of earthly witness to establish heavenly truths,—fitly closes the record of St John. The faith in the Lord's Divinity which the Evangelist had proclaimed in his own words at
John i. 1. the beginning is now shewn at the end to have been reached by disciples in actual intercourse with the living Lord, and reached through doubts fearlessly met. For each doubt of St Thomas was in

the end fully justified, while each was shewn to lead to a higher and an unexpected truth. The disciples did die with Christ, die to old hopes, but only to rise again to newness of life. They did not know the way, the way of perfect self-surrender, but it was made clear to them from the Cross. No testimony could prove that of which sense is no measure; but through this admission the authority of the spirit to interpret the partial teaching of facts was solemnly vindicated. And so in the end there is opened the prospect of a still happier triumph for a later time. *Jesus saith unto him Because thou hast seen me, thou hast believed: blessed are they that have not seen and yet have believed.* *Blessed are they that have not seen and yet have believed.* This is the last and greatest of the Beatitudes: the special heritage which Christ left for those who should come after. This is the Beatitude which is offered again to us all in the prospect of Christmas. First there is the hearing of the ear, and then the seeing with the eye, the eye of the heart, and we fall before the Incarnate Word in humility and adoration and faith.

V.

WAITING. (St John.)

If I will that he tarry till I come, what is that to thee?

St John xxi. 22.

V. *WAITING.*

AMONG the apostles of the Lord there is no one to whom we turn with the same affectionate and trustful reverence as to St John whom we commemorate to-day. We seem to know him with something of a sympathetic knowledge. He brings the Lord's love near to us in a peculiar way. There is in St Peter a far keener energy of decisive action. There is in St Paul a larger sweep of thought. But in St John there is what to us now is still more precious, a calm strength, a power of spiritual vision which looks on all the riddles and sorrows of life, and looks through them, though it cannot arrange in familiar forms the glory which it sees beyond. The characteristic of St John is 'waiting'; and I think that it will be useful for us to meditate on this grace of 'waiting' for a few minutes, as it is seen in *the disciple whom Jesus loved.* APPEND. V.

John xiii. 23; xix. 26; xxi. 7, 20. Contrast xx. 2.

The characteristic comes out very plainly in the last chapter of his Gospel. It is shewn in St John's own act: it is shewn by the Lord's

APPEND. V. John xxi. 7 ff. words. St John with the instinct of love discovered that the stranger who had mysteriously blessed the apostles' unfruitful work must be the Lord; but when St Peter, taking up the conviction from him, flung himself into the water to reach without delay the Lord whom he had found, St John waited till in the natural order he was borne to Him, waited in the fulfilment of the duty which belonged to him, waited to secure the gift which had been received. John xxi. 20 ff. And so afterwards, when a threefold commission had restored to St Peter his promised work, and dark hints of martyrdom had been added as the close, and all had been summed up by the Lord in the words *Follow Me,* St John silently waited to hear if for him there would be any light upon the future. He silently waited, and St Peter put his thought into words broken and incomplete. He *saith to Jesus, Lord, and this man, what?* what shall he do? what shall he suffer? what shall be his part in the chequered scene of labour and sorrow which fills the period of Thy absence? *Jesus saith unto him, If I will that he tarry till I come, what is that to thee?* if I will that he wait, and fulfil his office by waiting and not by following?

They also serve who only stand and wait.

And so indeed from first to last St John did fulfil his work by waiting. He waited on the threshold of life, in the circle of the Baptist's disciples, pondering thoughts which the great herald could stir but could not satisfy, till the decisive sign was given and by that he knew *the Lamb of God.* APPEND. V. John i. 35 ff.

He waited by the Cross, waited perhaps through that awful darkness of three hours, and then he heard the words which set the seal on his devotion, when the Lord *saith to His mother Woman, behold, thy son!*; and *to the disciple Behold, thy mother!* John xix. 26 f.

This sacred charge again imposed on St John the duty of waiting. If others could go from city to city bearing the message of the King, it was his place to sit still: to sit still and, in reverent and watchful communion with her who became his mother, look into those awful depths which in after years he opened to the Church.

One by one the apostolic band passed away, some by martyrdom, some by silent and unnoticed death. The Holy City was laid desolate: the Sanctuary was overthrown for ever. And St John waited still, a stranger in a new age. He waited, and after waiting the full time he had his work to do. Then his Gospel could be written, for all ages, as one of our great poets has told us:

> Since much that at the first, in deed and word,
> Lay simply and sufficiently exposed,

APPEND. V.

> Had grown (or else [his] soul was grown to match,
> Fed through such years, familiar with such light,
> Guarded and guided still to see and speak)
> Of new significance and fresh result;
> What first were guessed as points [he then] knew stars
> And named them...

And even when this last work was done and he was laid to rest, there was a strange legend widely current that he was waiting still, asleep but not dead in his grave at Ephesus, and men thought that they saw the dust move above the spot where he lay, stirred by the breath of the saint. It is a wild, fantastic story, but yet it enshrines a truth. For spiritually St John is waiting now, waiting for men to learn that message of love which life is given us to learn, and which lies, clothed with a power of glory that it has not yet entered into the heart of man to realise, in the fact that *the Word became flesh.*

'Waiting': in the history of the apostle we can see how the discipline was blessed, blessed for him who was so brought ever nearer and nearer to God, blessed for the people whom he served: blessed when he was bidden to leave his first teacher: blessed when he was kept back from the enterprise of missionary service: blessed when he was left the solitary survivor of an old world, weary and yet joyful to bear 'the burthen of the latest time'.

And is not all this, brethren, a parable of life for us? Can we not feel that it is well for us to pause and think of the blessedness of 'waiting', hurried, as we are, to and fro, by the inevitable tumult of modern life? For it is still through long watching that at last the opportunity is found for mastering the truth towards which our hopes have been turned. It is still not unfrequently through sorrow that we gain little by little the power of insight by which the meaning of familiar facts is disclosed. It is still by silent ponderings, in the solitude of the inner chamber or in the solitude of the crowd, that we learn the lesson of communing with God. And our anxiety for results which we can measure, our restlessness under conditions which we hold to be unfavourable to our progress, our passion for excitement, tend to deprive us of these highest fruits of life. We cannot remove the conditions under which our work is to be done but we can transform them. They are the elements out of which we must build the temples wherein we serve.

In one sense God gives nothing, while in another sense He gives all things. He requires us, that is, to make His gifts our own by using the power which He inspires. Not all at once and not as we should have expected, and not without

APPEND. V. many delays, does that which indeed is ours become ours.

So it is that waiting itself becomes a work; and of all the promises of Scripture none, I think, speaks with fuller encouragement to such as seem to find no fruit of labour or no scope for it, if only they wait for the Lord Who will not leave the desolate, than this: *In your patience ye shall win your souls.* (Luke xxi. 19.)

That is the benediction of waiting; the blessing of this day's Festival.